A VIEW FROM BENEATH
THE DANCING ELEPHANT

Also by Peter E. Greulich

The World's Greatest Salesman
An IBM Caretaker's Perspective: Looking Back

Democracy in Business
Volume I of Tom Watson Sr. Essays on Leadership

We Are All Assistants
Volume II of Tom Watson Sr. Essays on Leadership

We Forgive Thoughtful Mistakes
Volume III of Tom Watson Sr. Essays on Leadership

A VIEW FROM

BENEATH

REDISCOVERING
IBM'S CORPORATE
CONSTITUTION

THE

DANCING

ELEPHANT

PETER E.
GREULICH

EDITED BY DAVID KASSIN FRIED

MBI Concepts Corporation • Austin, Texas USA

RESPECT, SERVICE AND EXCELLENCE

Printed in the United States of America.

MBI Concepts Corporation books and articles may be tailored for business, educational or sales promotion use. Please contact MBI Concepts Corporation for further information at info@mbiconcepts.com.

Excerpts from *Men—Minutes—Money* and *Thirty Years of Management Briefings* reprinted with permission of IBM. Such permission should not be construed to mean that IBM approves of this book.

Names of IBM employees and some event locations have been changed.

20 19 18 17 16 15 14   1 2 3 4 5

ISBN-13: 978-0-9833734-6-9   (paperback)
ISBN-10: 0-9833734-6-9   (paperback)

ISBN-13: 978-0-9833734-7-6   (electronic publication for Amazon Kindle)
ISBN-10: 0-9833734-7-7

ISBN-13: 978-0-9833734-8-3   (electronic publication for iTunes, Google and Barnes and Noble)
ISBN-10: 0-9833734-8-5

Library of Congress Control Number: 2013918799

Greulich, Peter Eugene, 1953–
    A View From Beneath the Dancing Elephant: Rediscovering IBM's Corporate Constitution / Peter E. Greulich
        p. cm.
    1. Management. 2. International Business Machines Corporation—History. 3. International Business Machines—Management. 4. Corporate turnarounds—United States—Case Studies. 5. Watson, Thomas John, 1874–1956. I. Title

Illustrations in Building Family, Building Excellence, Extending the Game Plan and Musical Chairs by Rivkah.

Redwood forest pictures provided by Mario D. Vaden, Photographer & Arborist.

Elephant photo on the cover: © Depositphotos.com/ kangarooarts.

Book Design by TLC Graphics, *www.TLCGraphics.com.*
Cover by Tamara Dever / Interior by Monica Thomas.

Edited by David Kassin Fried.

For Thomas J. Watson Sr.,
Thomas J. Watson Jr.,
and Tom,
who took a chance and hired
a political science major into their IBM.

CONTENTS

" The modern business enterprise is not just an economic institution. In order to discharge its economic function, it has to have a concept behind it, an organization and a constitution. It is a social institution and a community as well, and needs to be managed — and studied — as such."[1]

Peter F. Drucker,
The Concept of the Corporation

PREFACE

❝ When we read we must always keep in mind that we are not reading just to get the conclusion of the writer, because if we do that we are just getting one man's view. We must read and keep in mind the fact that we are reading to stimulate our own thoughts; we should take the points and the ideas and the suggestions that we get from this reading and apply them in our own way and in our own work. Never accept any man's conclusions until you have analyzed them and found them acceptable. It is so easy to be carried away by something that sounds good, something that a man with the gift of oratory may present convincingly. Analyze it thoroughly. Assimilate it. Make it your own."[2]

Thomas J. Watson Sr., *Men — Minutes — Money*

If the Watsons still ran IBM, this book would never have seen the light of day. I would have mailed it directly to Tom Watson Sr. or his son and then retired knowing they would act. Unfortunately, IBM's twenty-first-century leadership, so far, has not inspired such trust and confidence. The twentieth-century IBM believed in the integrity of the individual. It created the world's first corporate constitution and defined global social responsibility. The twenty-first-century IBM has misplaced all of these and has lost its culture, its constitution and its way.

IBM stands as one of the world's most representative corporate social ecologies. If it were a city, its representation from 175 countries would make it one of the world's most educated and ethnically diverse. Its population would place it in the top forty cities of the United States and Brazil, the top ten of Malaysia, the top five of France and the top two of Romania or Norway.

In the short time frame from conception to realization of this book, this corporate metropolis expanded 19%, from 341,279 employees to 405,535, then contracted 31% to 278,039, only to grow again by 68% to a historic peak of 466,995.[3] The strain this would put on any social infrastructure is unimaginable.

Therefore, although economics may write headlines, we must push past just an economic evaluation. It was a century-old social network that held IBM together, and that's what we must study to assess its future.

Although my opinion is only one of many, I have interviewed thousands of IBM employees over my thirty-year IBM career. We are an opinionated bunch, and our perspectives on change at IBM are as diverse as the company is old. I dislike stereotypes, and I believe the only true generalization is that all generalizations are false; but there are similarities in IBMers' views.

The elder generation retired before the mid-nineties. Its members had long careers and experienced the IBM Basic Beliefs as the Watsons intended. This generation's CEOs culturally imbedded the IBM Basic Beliefs through Open Doors, Speak Up!s, Executive Interviews, Opinion Surveys and exemplary first-line management training. These IBMers had most of their retirement invested in IBM stock and its defined-benefit pension plan, and they were grateful that Louis V. Gerstner Jr. took over for John Akers as CEO, because IBM's corporate bankruptcy would have meant their personal bankruptcy. When they hear the newest generation of IBMers caution others to think carefully before adding IBM to their employment short list, many wonder why.

The transition generation was hired in the late sixties to mid-eighties. Tom Watson Jr. still wandered the halls of Armonk, talking directly with many of them. They have experienced a range of IBM leaders, good and bad: from Watson Jr., Learson and Cary, to Opel, Akers, Gerstner, Palmisano and Rometty. An adaptable group, this generation includes everyone from those who built the first mainframe to those hired to construct the Hundred Billion Dollar IBM. They have experienced the Basic Beliefs, but also the ongoing changes in pension and health benefits, resource actions and financial impacts around IBM's earnings-per-share road maps. Some have survived thirty-plus years like the elder generation, but most have not.

The younger generation joined after the IBM recovery in the early nineties, and they have never experienced the IBM Basic Beliefs except on isolated teams. Many accept as fact what Gerstner wrote in *Who Says Elephants Can't Dance?*—that "Respect for the Individual came to mean that an IBMer could do pretty much anything he or she wanted to do, within the broad HR and legal rulebooks, with little or no accountability."[4] They see the new corporate workplace as just a fact of life: many corporations have quarterly resource actions, minimal pay increases, regular job-hopping and little correlation between pay and performance. Why expect anything different? They view the Watsons' IBM as an archaic, wistful dream of old men.

Once upon a time, IBM's Basic Beliefs were the corporate constitution that bounded all of Big Blue's decisions. The elder generation sees them as principles that encouraged independent thought and empowered action. The new generation, if they are even aware of them, sees them as nice words and not much else. The transition generation lives with their loss.

This book is just one perspective, humbly offered, from a member of the transition generation.

Peter F. Drucker once leveraged an eighteen-month study of General Motors to become one of the preeminent management philosophers of the twentieth century. Decades earlier, Tom Watson Sr. had already utilized an uncanny sense of community to achieve the same ends. I offer the insights in this book as an addendum to Drucker's work because we need more servants of business—and fewer masters.

Change occurs slowly in a society of a half million people. It may impact one generation but not the next; it may affect one geography and no other; or it may divide executive and employee. But universally, the Basic Beliefs no longer unite generations of IBMers. This is the century's most significant change.

Endnotes

1 Peter F. Drucker, *The Concept of the Corporation* (New American Library, New York, 1964), p. xii Preface.

2 Thomas J. Watson Sr., *Men—Minutes—Money*, (IBM Corporation, New York, 1934), pp. 25, 42, reprinted with permission of IBM.

3 Any reference to the number of IBM employees and data that is dependent on this number (such as revenue per employee) uses IBM annual report information and includes

complementary employees. A complementary employee is an approximation of an equivalent full-time employee hired under a temporary, part-time and limited-term employment arrangement to meet specific business needs in a flexible and cost-effective manner.

4 Louis V. Gerstner Jr., *Who Says Elephants Can't Dance?* (Harper Business, New York, 2002), p. 186.

INTRODUCTION

> 💬 History treats what happens on the surface. "ISMs"—that is the philosophical systems — may be called the atmosphere, but society is the ecology."[1]
>
> **Peter F. Drucker,**
> *The End of Economic Man*

A Resilient Social Ecology

There is no more majestic tree in all of North America than the coastal redwood. It soars fifteen stories above the main dome of the Taj Mahal, climbs seven stories beyond the torch of the Statue of Liberty and scales to one-third the height of the Eiffel Tower.

Mario D. Vaden, Photographer & Arborist

If a lone redwood were illuminated against a backdrop of the Washington Monument, its shadow would ascend two-thirds the height of the stone monolith. But unlike the Washington Monument, which requires a foundation four stories deep, the coastal redwood's root system only skims along the first four to six feet of the earth's surface—barely the height of an average man. These leviathans are the most top-heavy of all creations, with a mass above ground that is ten times the mass below. For all their majesty, nature's most gentle breeze would eventually topple a solitary giant.

With a root system running only six feet deep, resiliency is found in community.

For the redwood, resiliency lies not in the grandeur of the individual tree but in the forest. The redwood's design is one of individual greatness interweaved with community. The trees' root systems scatter in all directions. They intertwine. They graft. They strengthen and stabilize one another. Interlocked, they withstand great winds. Together they reduce the effects of erosion and increase the odds of survival. As every season begins, it is the forest that withstands nature's relentless, repetitive and continual assaults. When great storms bring devastating winds in from the sea and pummel the land, genetically weaker trees collapse into mounds of debris, but the redwood forest does not yield.

When the summer brings relentless drying heat, and the underbrush becomes dry tinder, the resulting fire will lap harmlessly against the redwoods' foot-thick bark. When torrential rains arrive, pushing landslides of smothering earth and debris into the valleys, lesser trees suffocate, but the redwoods breathe through ever-rising networks of horizontal roots—sometimes overcoming up to three stories of engulfing soil. When insects tunnel deep into open wounds to reproduce and devastate whole sections of less adaptable forests, the redwoods block every assault, as insects are nothing but a minor nuisance. And when forests everywhere are damaged, the redwoods take advantage through cloning: new sprouts arise from seemingly devastated stumps, heavily damaged trees unleash saplings from their underlying root systems, and fallen giants push their upward-facing branches skyward. In the first five years, these clones will stand fifteen times taller than other types of trees. The community raises the individual in splendor far above its competitors; and the individual redwood extends the majesty of its surrounding forest. They are indistinguishably bound together through a common DNA—a single sixty-six chromosome organism that presents as much genetic diversity against pests and pathogens as an entire field of genetically diverse wildflowers.[2]

Because of the redwood forest's ecosystem, individual trees have survived for more than two millennia. Today's mightiest redwood sprang from the ground as the Great Wall extended across China; it ascended above the hilltops with the construction of the Roman Colosseum; and it ruled the forest before the completion of the minarets of the Blue Mosque. It was present when we set foot on the moon; it will still be present when man strides across another planet. We wonder at the majesty of a lone tree, but we should stand in awe of the resiliency, longevity and strength provided by its forest.

The Redwood Forest of Corporate America

For most of the twentieth century, IBM was the redwood forest of corporate America. The Watsons, as true leaders, buried deep in the heart of their company a belief system that transcended their limited time in power. They studied mankind. They understood it. They captured our dreams, hopes, aspirations and desire to be part of something greater—to be part of a dynamic team. Where others saw employees moving uncaringly between corporations, the Watsons' vision for their business was always to be more.

They ensured a century of resiliency through a loyal, dedicated and enthusiastic team. They desired their corporation to evolve, but only within the context of a preeminent belief system that would reach across decades and across leaders. This unifying culture was framed in the recession of 1921,

Mario D. Vaden, Photographer & Arborist

IBM's twentieth-century leadership only desired to stand tall in our midst.

stressed during the Great Depression and has proven to work through thirteen recessions since.

Thomas J. Watson Sr. lived his belief system. He communicated it through maxims, modeled it for his executives and established it as the foundation for the future. He demanded adherence from his entire management team and from anyone who wanted to carry the title of IBMer. Thomas J. Watson Jr. captured his father's maxims, wrote them down, reinforced them, modernized and proselytized for them. He carried them into every cubicle, manufacturing shop and business relationship. It was these beliefs that defeated the competition and withstood economic storms. If there was ever a true IBM monopoly, it was this overpowering cultural monopoly founded on the IBM Basic Beliefs.

Summarizing the power of this belief system, Tom Watson Jr. once said:

> Consider any great organization—one that has lasted over the years—and I think you will find that it owes its resiliency not to its form of organization or administrative skills, but to the power of what we call beliefs and the appeal these beliefs have for its people. This, then, is my thesis: I firmly believe that any organization, in order to survive and

achieve success, must have a sound set of beliefs on which it premises all its policies and actions.[3]

T. Vincent Learson, the first non-Watson CEO, leaned on these beliefs when the company faced the third largest stock market decline in history (see Appendix A). He wrote to his management team:

> You know as well as I that these are difficult times for IBM. The fact that this is a temporary situation — although when it will end we do not know — hardly eases the apprehension of employees who see things happening that they have not experienced before. They are being asked to work harder at a time when budgets are tight and promotion opportunities are fewer. Many are being inconvenienced by being asked to take different jobs or relocate. All of these things are necessary.... The success of IBM always has been and will be based on its people. They have amply demonstrated their willingness to devote all their talents and skills to their company. You and I owe them skilled, understanding leadership for this is a proud, hard-hitting team — the best in the world — and we must keep it that way.[4]

Just as the redwood's genetic material ensures consistency across generations, the Basic Beliefs once connected generations of IBMers and their leaders. The Beliefs were adaptable in almost every way, except as a core set of immovable, unbendable and unbreakable values. They made us a family.

I personally experienced the Basic Beliefs during economically difficult times. In the recession of the eighties, administrators were fast becoming obsolete. Personal computers replaced word processing centers and automated order entry systems displaced old jobs — including my management position. We were encouraged to move into support roles that provided higher value to our customers. It was technically and personally difficult. I spent months away from my wife and children, but my IBM family was always there to provide support and encouragement — they adapted my training around the birth of a son. Over my thirty-year career, in the midst of suffocating industry change, I would over and over again be challenged to send out new lateral roots. It was always an individual decision to accept the challenge, but the individual found strength and encouragement in community.

An Ecology in Decline

In the late nineties, the very foundation of the IBM forest came under attack. The company moved from a living, breathing organism composed of IBMers to a company of IBM employees. Individual trees fell all around us. Our incredible, intertwining roots were ripped from the soil, the once solid earth uprooted and scattered skyward.

During that time the Watsons' original spirit, vision and passion faded. It could only be found in isolated teams led by strong leaders. Individuals were removed from the forest and planted in home offices. For survival, they put down individually deep roots. Many worked to pad their résumés—mobile, transient employees on their way to somewhere else. International teams became dysfunctional, as there were endless ways to communicate but—with the loss of the Basic Beliefs—fewer ways to reach consensus.

Much of this was done in the name of remaining competitive, of being more nimble and adaptable to changing market conditions. Some interpret being faster, moving quicker or implementing change as abandoning old tenets—discarding what seem, to them, archaic beliefs. But the Watsons were willing to change everything *except* their most fundamental and basic principles. I believe, from everything recorded about Tom Watson Sr. and his son, that they would be most reflective on the new IBM. They would not admire the black ink on a balance sheet, the sheer size of their corporation or the record earnings per share. These would be important—they set expectations beyond those of any corporation in existence today—but they would not celebrate the profits that came at the expense of IBM's culture.

This new path brought with it a new attitude: "This is not your father's IBM." Even Louis V. Gerstner Jr., to his credit, acknowledges in *Who Says Elephants Can't Dance?* that IBM is more than just a financial entity. He foresaw, perhaps with apprehension, a herculean effort:

> Frankly, if I could have chosen not to tackle the IBM culture head-on, I probably wouldn't have. For one thing, my bias coming in was toward strategy, analysis, and measurement. I'd already been successful with those, and like anyone, I was inclined to stick with what had worked for me earlier in my career. Once I found a handful of smart people, I knew we could take a fresh look at the business and make good strategic calls or invest in new businesses or get the cost structure in shape. In comparison, changing the attitude and behavior of hundreds of thousands of people is very, very hard to accomplish. Business schools don't teach you how to do it.[5]

It is a fact that IBM's culture had drifted; but it is also a fact that when Mr. Gerstner arrived it was broken, not dead. Rather than changing it, he could have considered himself to be in what Tom Watson Sr. called a practical business school — the company that defined the term surrounded him. For eight decades this society had inspired a positive employee attitude while demanding disciplined behavior.

When Gerstner wrote that the "most corrupted" of all the IBM Basic Beliefs was respect for the individual,[6] it hit us as if the President of the United States had written that we should no longer pursue a more perfect union. Surely a century-old corporation, like a two-century-old nation, is more than its founding words. But great leaders do not seek to abolish a people's constitution; rather they seek a return to its original intent. Lou Gerstner would have found the answers if he had dug deeper.

He just needed the humility to be a student of The IBM.

IBM's Twentieth-Century Corporate Constitution

> The [U.S.] Constitution is not a "plan" of government.... Neither is it "pragmatic." It establishes a few, simple organs of government with enormous powers of which only the limits are given.... The purpose of such a concept is never to serve as a rigid rule. Rather it is to be used like a compass bearing taken across rugged mountains. The actual trail will follow the natural contours of the terrain; but the bearing will give the deviation from the true course at every step and will thus ultimately

lead to the objective, however great the detour and however much the objective has been lost sight of on the way.[7]

Peter F. Drucker, *The Concept of the Corporation*

My daughter teaches her kindergarten class three basic tenets: be respectful, be kind and be neat. The twentieth-century IBM used three basic beliefs to socialize and create the first corporate employee-owners. This belief system bound us together, ensured right over might and encouraged individual thought and action. The Beliefs were IBM's heart and soul and kept it on course. They were its economic engine, powering change through eighteen recessions and the Great Depression. Because of them, coffee grinders, meat slicers, time clocks and tabulating machines evolved into mainframes and information processing.

Any individual, department chief or corporate head could be all-powerful as long as he or she remained within the Basic Beliefs' boundaries. The Basic Beliefs were not a detailed plan for success, and neither were they pragmatic; yet when Tom Watson Jr. wrote them, he believed that *we must be ready to change everything about ourselves except these beliefs.*[8]

These three words established IBM's Corporate Constitution:

Respect for the Individual[9]

Our basic belief is respect for the individual, for his rights and dignity. It follows from this principle that IBM should:

- *Help each employee to develop his potential and make the best use of his abilities.*

- *Pay and promote on merit.*

- *Maintain two-way communications between manager and employee, with opportunity for a fair hearing and equitable settlement of disagreements.*

Respect was true north. It was never the objective and it was rarely the direction traveled, but rather it was the place from which everyone oriented him- or herself on the corporate topographical map—that immovable reference point for setting one's personal compass.

Respect transcended color, creed, sex, national origin and sexual orientation. It was about accepting the different backgrounds, viewpoints, temperaments and abilities of thousands of unique personalities. It was about maintaining harmony between all these individuals that make up a corporation. Today, the politically correct term is diversity, but Respect for the Individual surpassed diversity by accepting each person's true uniqueness: it was easier to accept another's strength or weakness, and it was also easier to remove those who failed to live up to the standard, when true Respect was in play.

Many may believe it impossible to achieve true Respect for all individuals, but IBMers believed it was not only attainable but attained, for both the individual and the corporation. Watson once told a room full of employees that if they would not associate with others because they thought they had better educational advantages, superior home surroundings or were from a better class, then IBM was not for them.[10] He went on to say that any policy in his business that was not good enough for every man was not a good policy for the business, and he would not adopt it.[11]

Thus, IBM's twentieth-century CEOs ensured that Respect for the Individual was at the heart of—and pervasive across—their corporation. As Watson once said, "We are just men—men standing together, shoulder to shoulder, all working for one common good; we have one common interest, and the good of each of us as individuals affects the greater good of the company."[12]

With this properly aligned compass it was possible to navigate deep personal valleys, clamber up steep corporate cliffs and have the tough but productive personnel conversations that made IBM great.

Service to the Customer [13]

We are dedicated to giving our customers the best possible service. Our products and services bring profits only to the degree that they serve the customer and satisfy his needs. This demands that we:

- *Know our customers' needs, and help them anticipate future needs.*

- *Help customers use our products and services in the best possible way.*

- *Provide superior equipment maintenance and supporting services.*

While Respect was true north, Service was the destination. Establishing an objective based on Service gave the individual purpose and the team focus; but when that objective was based on *True* Service, something magnificent happened—a family spirit evolved.

In a capitalistic system profits are a necessity: they improve products, pay dividends, print paychecks, provide benefits and safeguard social stability. Profits also distribute resources: those that are in low demand are cheap, and those that are in high demand are expensive. This method of allocating resources creates a natural tension between rewarding individual potential and shielding the individual from the impact of catastrophes beyond his or her control—such as terminal illness and natural or economic disasters. It is these tensions that a caring capitalistic society must resolve. Spend a few too many dollars and corporate bankruptcy will quickly fill the financial pages; but failing to act ethically will bankrupt the corporate spirit and eventually fill a scholarly work. Either way, the corporation will find itself in the elephant graveyard.

As Jim Collins wrote in *Built to Last*, "Profit is like oxygen, food, water, and blood for the body; they are not the *point* of life, but without them, there is no life."[14] Corporations maintain life through profits; but find purpose and permanence in True Service—the equitable distribution of those profits between their four stakeholders: customers, shareholders, employees and society. So although it is the CEO's responsibility to make a profit, it is his or her ultimate responsibility to reach beyond service and attain True Service.

Many confuse caring, the emotional center of True Service, with paternalism. These two could not be more different. According to Watson:

> In attempting to counsel or advise those whom we employ, we must not adopt a paternal attitude.... When independent thought and action should be the order of the day, employees resent an attitude of paternalism. It is a well-known fact, however, that an employee's efficiency suffers if his mind is ill at ease, and that worry over financial troubles is one of the most powerful sources for the destruction of mental peace.[15]

Paternalism creates dependence by restricting a person's responsibilities and freedoms, supposedly in his or her best interest. But this only breeds resentment and inefficiency. To ensure that caring doesn't take on the controlling aspect of paternalism requires constant attention, but the hue and cry of paternalism should never inhibit a society from caring.

Tom Watson Sr. built his corporation on *True* Service — rendering service beyond the thought of personal gain.[16] Ever the believer in individual reward for individual performance, he achieved balance by creating a corporate family spirit.

The twentieth-century IBM, even in the most desperate of economic times, aligned personal, corporate and stakeholder objectives. In the Great Depression, Watson explained to his sales team that he could not pay them what they deserved because it was the company's duty to pay shareholders a dividend. Later, (for reasons I'll explain in the next chapter) he did the opposite, and explained to shareholders why he raised employee benefits instead of increasing dividends. In all cases he used True Service to align everyone's objectives.

Every IBMer by definition was a Service man: to customers, shareholders, society, each other and even himself.

Excellence Must Be a Way of Life [17]

We want IBM to be known for its excellence. Therefore, we believe that every task, in every part of the business, should be performed in a superior manner and to the best of our ability. Nothing should be left to chance in our pursuit of excellence. For example, we must:

- *Lead in new developments.*

- *Be aware of advances made by others, better them where we can, or be willing to adopt them whenever they fit our needs.*

- *Produce quality products of the most advanced design and at the lowest possible cost.*

While Respect for the Individual ensured that alternate and even divergent paths were considered, and while True Service determined the objective, it was the pursuit of Excellence that ensured that change was continual, sustained and culturally ingrained. Through the pursuit of Excellence IBMers sought out the best path. It was the agent of change, forcing us to continually evaluate whether we were as great as we could be and how to be better.

In this system, "centralized excellence" was an oxymoron. Centralization assumes that one set of individuals can determine the best paths for the multitude. It is an attempt by headquarters to think for the individual no matter the uniqueness of the situation. At best this minimizes risk and results in a win *most* of the time. But whether you're a salesman dealing with a dissatisfied customer or a teacher dealing with a discouraged student or a social worker assisting a homeless family, the only way to achieve consistent organizational Excellence is to empower the individual to cross, if necessary, difficult personal or corporate terrain. Therefore, the CEO's responsibility is to empower the standard bearer of

Excellence—the individual—and encourage their forward movement. As Watson Sr. said:

> The success of IBM does not, never has and never will depend upon me or my immediate associates. The success of IBM depends upon the spirit, the thought and the effort of each individual in the business. It is because of the spirit, the thought and the effort of IBM people that we have been moving forward and having a little success. It is because the individual IBM employee has the spirit and is willing to make individual contributions, rather than wait for the head of the business or the chief executives to tell him what to do about his work.[18]

When thousands of individuals practice Respect, Service, and Excellence, the number of potential paths becomes infinite. Creativity blossoms in these environments. Some ideas will succeed, some will fail, some will never see the light of day; but Excellence will emerge from the swarm of out-of-the-box thoughts. The focus is never on the route (unless that route violates a Basic Belief) but on achieving the objective. The result is thousands of employees who believe in individual thought and action.

They become employee-owners.

The Goal — Individual Thought and Individual Action

> Individual thought is very important. With our wonderful newspaper system, our magazines, the radio, etc., disseminating news every hour of the day, we are likely to get into a channel and all think about the same on every subject. It seems to me that what individual businesses of this country need is more individual thinking and action. The success of every business in working out of this depression and carrying on depends more on what we do as individuals than on anything else.... We have gone beyond the point where we can depend on any one man to think for us or to lead us all to success. So let us make up our minds to spread the doctrine of individual leadership and individual thinking.... Let us start with individual action right now.[19]
>
> **Thomas J. Watson Sr.**

IBM's Corporate Constitution
The Basic Beliefs

There was no other goal behind IBM's Corporate Constitution than individual thought and individual action. If the individual saw a wrong, he or she righted it; if the individual saw poor leadership, he or she confronted it; if there was inefficiency, the individual fixed it. Centralization of decision-making produces inefficiencies and conformity; decentralization of decision-making without a constitution produces chaos. The goal of putting all these beliefs together as an American Corporate Constitution was to *encourage* independent thought and *embolden* individual action while keeping individuals aligned around common objectives.

Life can, at times, challenge a corporation. Leaders will make mistakes. True employee-owners understand that their leadership is fallible. We accept that fallibility if our leaders have the insight to admit mistakes and learn from them. Watson's temper was known to be brutal, but his concern was overwhelmingly genuine. When he apologized for his outbursts, he often went not just to the employee-owner, but to his or her spouse and family. Leaders, too, are finding their way through a personal wilderness. When we use the same true north, then we are aligned, pursuing a joint objective and searching out the best path across difficult terrain.

The twentieth-century IBM traversed a demanding economic landscape, but it came through by returning over and over again to its Basic

Beliefs—its Corporate Constitution—to inspire individual thought and individual action. When Watson Jr. looked back on his corporation many years later, he said, "Strong beliefs win strong men and then make them stronger and as men become stronger so do the organizations to which they belong."[20]

Endnotes

1   Peter F. Drucker, *The End of Economic Man* (Transaction Publishers, New Brunswick and London, 2009), p. xii.

2   M. R. Ahuja and David B. Neale, "Origins of Polyploidy in Coast Redwood and Relationship of Coast Redwood to Other Genera of Taxodiaceae," *Silvae Genetica*, Vol. 51 (2–3), pp. 93–100.

3   Thomas J. Watson Jr., *A Business and Its Beliefs* (McGraw-Hill Book Company, Inc., New York, Toronto, London, 1963), p. 5.

4   T. Vincent Learson, *Thirty Years of Management Briefings* (IBM Corporation, Armonk, New York, 1988), p. 155, reprinted with permission of IBM.

5   Louis V. Gerstner, Jr., *Who Says Elephants Can't Dance?* (Harper Business, New York, 2002), p. 187.

6   Ibid., p. 186.

7   Peter F. Drucker, *The Concept of the Corporation* (New American Library, 1964) p. 71.

8   Thomas J. Watson Jr., *A Business and Its Beliefs* (McGraw-Hill Book Company, Inc., New York, Toronto, London, 1963), p. 5.

9   Thomas J. Watson Jr., *Thirty Years of Management Briefings* (IBM Corporation, Armonk, New York, 1988), pp. 128–131, reprinted with permission of IBM.

10 Peter E. Greulich, *The World's Greatest Salesman* (MBI Concepts Corporation, Austin, Texas, 2011), p. 15.

11 Ibid., p. 14.

12 Thomas J. Watson, *Men—Minutes—Money* (IBM Corporation, New York, 1934), p. 18, reprinted with permission of IBM.

13 Thomas J. Watson Jr., *Thirty Years of Management Briefings* (IBM Corporation, Armonk, New York, 1988), pp. 128–131, reprinted with permission of IBM.

14 James C. Collins and Jerry I. Porras, *Built to Last: Successful Habits of Visionary Companies* (Harper Business, New York, 1994), p. 55.

15 Peter E. Greulich, *The World's Greatest Salesman* (MBI Concepts Corporation, Austin, Texas, 2011), p. 302.

16 Peter E. Greulich, *Democracy in Business* (MBI Concepts Corporation, Austin, Texas, 2011), p. 58.

17 Thomas J. Watson Jr., *Thirty Years of Management Briefings* (IBM Corporation, Armonk, New York, 1988), pp. 128–131, reprinted with permission of IBM.

18 Peter E. Greulich, *The World's Greatest Salesman* (MBI Concepts Corporation, Austin, Texas, 2011), p. 279.

19 Ibid., p. 181.

20 Thomas J. Watson Jr., *A Business and Its Beliefs* (McGraw-Hill Book Company, Inc., New York, Toronto, London, 1963), p. 73.

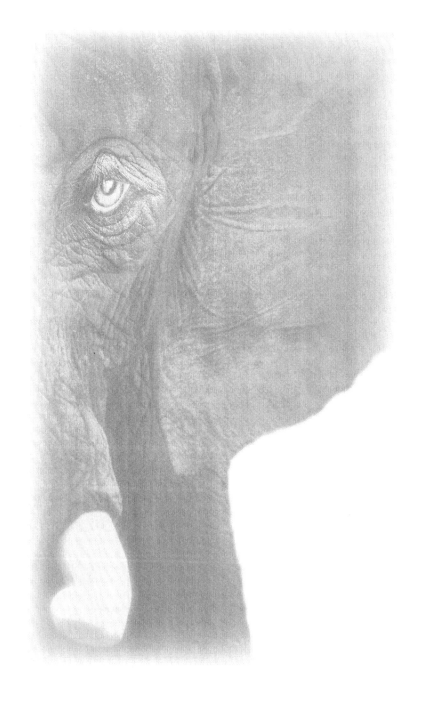

CHAPTER ONE

THE PATH TO GROWTH

> Business exists to provide a service to man: service to consumer man, to worker man, to investor man, and to the community of man."[1]
>
> **THINK**, Memorial Issue on Thomas John Watson

A Test of Character

Tom Watson's route to CEO of the Computing-Tabulating-Recording Company (C-T-R) was a path most men would have avoided and fewer still could have survived. Prior to joining C-T-R, Watson had worked at National Cash Register (NCR),[2] where he was indicted and convicted—along with his CEO, John Patterson, and twenty-seven others—of violating the Sherman Antitrust Act (see Appendix B). He was subsequently fired. Six months later, in May 1914, C-T-R's founder Charles Flint hired him, only to have the board of directors hold

> **IBM's Historical Naming**
>
> The Computing-Tabulating-Recording Company (C-T-R) was IBM's predecessor.
>
> - In 1911, Charles R. Flint forms C-T-R Company.
> - In 1914, Tom Watson Sr. took charge.
> - In 1917, C-T-R Canada was renamed International Business Machines (IBM).
> - In 1923, IBM name was applied to C-T-R Latin America.
> - In 1924, IBM replaced C-T-R name worldwide.

back the title of president pending resolution of the NCR antitrust case. That would take two years: one for the Appeals Court to rule in favor of the defendants,* and a second for the government to finally drop it (after the Supreme Court refused to hear arguments). In the midst of this personal turmoil, C-T-R was deep in debt and facing the end of a two-year-long recession.†

So when Watson stood to speak before his salesmen for the first time, they were anxious about their futures. Their company was on the brink of failure, and their last hope for financial success was a convicted criminal with no title on his business card—a national symbol of unfair competition. His character had been questioned by the newspapers, and

---

* There were three counts brought to court. The Appeals Court dismissed two of them and ruled evidence on the remaining count insufficient. At this point the board, believing that the case would eventually be dropped, made Watson the president and general manager.

† When founded, the company started with an aggregate bonded indebtedness of three times its current assets. By 1914 the interest charges ($405,874) were almost equal to net earnings ($489,861), and $10 million in stock had a market value of less than $3 million.

they questioned it, too. So when Watson finished speaking, there was no applause. Just silence and skepticism.

One man gave voice to the multitude, commenting, "Perhaps, the past holds more than the future."[3] It would have been a crisis of confidence for any man, but Tom Watson did not leave. He waited. He wanted someone to bring up the elephant in the room.‡

It wasn't until later in the meeting that one of the salesmen asked the question Watson had been waiting for — about fairness and competition. Their new leader strode back up to the front of the room, interrupting the meeting and taking charge:

> You know, gentlemen, it is bad policy to do anything unfair with anybody, anywhere, at any time, in business or outside of business. No man ever won except in the one honest, fair and square way in which you men are working.[4]

The room burst into applause. More applause would interrupt him again and again as Watson discussed fairness beyond just competition in business — he discussed his beliefs and displayed his internal character. In the years to follow he would often say, "Reputation is what people think you are; character is what you really are; what you know yourself to be."[5] IBM's character was now rooted in a man who had come as close to death in the business world as one possibly could and survive; and his standards of business conduct would ensure that IBM never faced a similar near-death experience.

Because he knew that very few customers would ever meet him or his executives, he hired salesmen who would live his belief system.[6] He built a corporation with an internal character that defined its outward reputation.

But from the outset it was not easy. He needed money to invest in competitive products for his salesmen, and his existing customers needed more value. Perhaps George F. Johnson — president of the Endicott-Johnson

---

‡ This is an important concept in this book, so for the benefit of any readers whose first language may not be English, an *elephant in the room* is an obvious truth that is being ignored or concealed.

Corporation and a longtime friend of Watson's—best summarized Watson's perspective: "Mere money has no brains, no part in management. All it is entitled to is security and a fair interest on the investment…. I don't believe that any man can own a business. It belongs to the customers, to the workers, to the community, to the public."[7]

Watson understood the difference between managing a company and managing a stock price. When he was hired, he told the C-T-R board of directors, "If you want me to come in here and operate this business for the benefit of the business, I'll do it, but I will not have anything to do with the operation of it from a stock standpoint."[8] To him, building a strong company was the best path to a stronger stock. So with the backing of C-T-R's founder, Flint—but over the objections of the shareholders—he suppressed dividends to put money back into the business.

Unfortunately, some on the board looked upon C-T-R as little more than a holding company:

> They had no sympathy for Watson's plans, which meant the sacrifice of immediate profits for the long-range benefit of the business. [Certain directors and some officers of the company] formed a secret stock pool, buying and selling stock to create the appearance of demand with an eye to boosting its price. Watson threatened to expose the conspiracy by taking his case directly to the press.[9]

This undertaking by officers of the company was legal in its time, but it was never ethical. Maybe because Watson was a "convicted criminal" awaiting an appeal, they thought he would look the other way. He chose not to. Here was a man under a cloud of suspicion for violating antitrust legalities standing in ethical opposition to a widely used practice of his day.

Watson believed that no man could ever hope to be a great leader if he did not develop a strong character, and C-T-R from the very beginning tested his.

A Bad Business Decision

Over the next seven years, Watson would grow the scale, tabulating and clock business. Net income quadrupled from $490,000 to $2.1 million. Optimistic by nature, Tom Watson was now ecstatic; but sometimes reality arrives even when the CEO least expects it:

> With sales at fifteen million dollars, Watson grandly set a growth objective of one hundred percent in one year—double the company's sales and production capacity. This walk-on-water confidence was fortified by a fine new tabulating machine plant on the flats of Endicott…. His earlier predictions of increased yearly growth, not only for the company, but for the American economy, held up for six heady years, but in the seventh—a famine year after the fat—they fell apart in the postwar panic of 1921, a short-term catastrophe that produced a nationwide wave of bankruptcies. In part by misfortune and in part by an uncharacteristic failure of Watson to remain in command of the facts about his own business, he was dealt a nearly mortal blow.[10]

The recession of 1921 was not a "short-term" catastrophe—some refer to it today as the Depression of 1920–21. It was a lengthy eighteen months comprising the fifth largest stock market decline in history.[11] Watson's optimism met the reality of an economy returning to normal after World War I, as well as the burst of an automotive bubble. C-T-R's net income would drop first by 11%, and then by 80%, to $331,000—one-third less than what it had been when he took charge seven years earlier. Bankruptcy was on the horizon.

So Watson took action. He cut all wages, including his salary, by 10%. His total income, because of its dependence on a profit-sharing formula, was reduced 40%—individual reward for individual effort cuts both ways, and he had endangered C-T-R's corporate viability. He laid off employees, with expensive, skilled labor going first—only four of fifty in the development department survived—which halted the production of a new printer needed by his customers. C-T-R would enter 1921 with 10% fewer employees than the year before.[12]

These actions were all justified. They were necessary to ensure corporate survival. Even so, they took their toll on the company.

But throughout, Watson demonstrated a tremendous desire to understand what that toll was — to see through the eyes of his employees. Kevin Maney writes of one such incident:

> In one meeting, Sam Hastings told Watson how hard it was to deliver the news of 10% salary cuts to workers already short of cash. He talked of one young woman making $16 per week and paying $10 dollars per week to live at the YWCA. For her, a cut of $1.60 per week "presented a real problem and the handling of such a situation as this was not a very pleasant task."[13]

Watson constantly practiced "Management by Wandering Around," more than a half century before Tom Peters would define the term in his book *In Search of Excellence*. To stay in touch, he spent precious hours with IBMers at Family Days, in sales branch offices, speaking at One Hundred Percent Clubs — a yearly sales recognition event for those achieving 100% of quota — and in informal one-on-one executive interviews. One IBMer remembers Watson showing up in the Roanoke, Virginia, sales office and asking about business while Mrs. Watson sat next to him and put on her lipstick. On their way to visit her personal family, this couple had taken the time to meet with their corporate family.[14] Today's corporate

Tom Watson Sr.'s Management by Wandering Around

1948 Annual Report

"We returned three weeks ago from a 6,500-mile trip through twelve states and the District of Columbia, on which we had the privilege of shaking hands and dining with 2,850 employees and their wives, representing forty-three IBM offices. This is in accordance with the custom we have followed since the beginning of our connection with the company. We enjoy it, for it permits us to become better acquainted with employees in our branch offices and it keeps us in close touch with activities in the field."

[In 1948 there were 19,000 U.S. employees. On this one trip, Mr. and Mrs. Watson saw fifteen percent of the IBM U.S. population.]

wisdom is to spend time with the customer; Watson spent time with his greatest asset—his salesmen.

C-T-R did weather this economic storm. By June 1923, the corporate debt was gone, there was a cash surplus of $1 million, and they could pay the full year's $6-per-share dividend from just the first six months' earnings.[15] That day the Board must have been glad that Watson won their 1914 ethical skirmish.

And yet for Watson the victory had been a Pyrrhic one. His corporation had survived, but he had made too many mistakes, and the cost had been too high. The $30 million sales goal he had set for 1921 was nowhere in sight—and wouldn't be met until 1937. He later said of this time, "I am ashamed of it....We did not have enough knowledge of what we ought to do....We had not given enough attention to our educational program. ...We threw up our hands with the rest of the country....We just didn't hang on to our courage and our belief in IBM and in IBM men."[16]

But the worst was yet to come—on the horizon was an economic downturn that would not be so forgiving of bad decisions. C-T-R's leader had learned some unexpected lessons, but would they be enough to guide him through the twentieth century's approaching darkest economic time?

The Roaring Twenties

In the 1920s, C-T-R became IBM and its net income climbed to $6,635,000—a twenty-fold increase. IBM paid dividends like clockwork. In 1925 it issued—in addition to its normal dividend—its first *stock* dividend,* of 20%. The next year IBM announced its first stock *split*—three for one—and followed that with two more stock dividends of 5% each.

Some investors, though, were putting these returns to shame. Though Watson had stopped IBM's officers from doing it in 1914, by the twenties it became an industry practice to pump and dump other companies' stock. Those in the know were making upward of 80% in one day, while

---

* A stock dividend is similar to a stock split—additional stock shares are distributed to shareholders that then earn cash dividends.

small investors lost everything. Although Watson couldn't have known the Great Depression was coming, he knew the economic system was sick. He would later comment about these times, "A certain group of people in the United States tried an experiment. They tried the experiment of making a fortune without working, of making a fortune through the stock exchange. They extended the experiment until it exploded and all went down to earth."[17]

He knew ethics wasn't enough. He needed financial controls.

In the early 1900s all corporate executives were receiving on-the-job training. The very concept of a corporation as a legal, economic and social institution was in its infancy, and the cadre of corporate EIEIOs—CFO, CIO, CTO, CMO, CSO, COO and CAO—available to today's twenty-first-century chief executive did not exist. So when Watson sought out a financial controller, he trained him in a truly Watson-esque style.

The man Watson hired, William F. Battin, spent his first year completely free of controller duties. He visited the factories, the home office and then—to understand the sales end of the business—every main sales office. He spoke at every sales convention: field sales conventions and annual sales events. When finished with his on-the-job training, he could stand in for any sales manager.

Quite simply, everyone in a Watson-run IBM—including the financial controller—was a salesman.[18]

Education, though, was not enough. Watson needed to align his team's priorities, so Tom, ever the showman, brought all his executives to the 1931 Hundred Percent Club. It was the who's who of his executive team facing his best-of-the-best salesmen. In his opening remarks he said:

> We did not ask these men [IBM executives] to come up here so that you might see how handsome they are, or just to hear them talk. That includes me. The reason they are here is that we want to give the men at headquarters an opportunity to look into the faces of the men who are most directly responsible for our company's progress.[19]

No one in Watson's IBM was going to lose faith in its people. His controller—now educated in sales and with the right priorities—would make every investment necessary to grow their business. And now that he was properly trained, Watson could trust him. (Nowhere is this trust more eloquently expressed than in the brevity of the Depression-era duty he assigned his controller: "Find ways to spend money."[20])

Meanwhile, Watson had come to believe that in the next economic downturn he would need a family of salesmen and a corporation aligned to support them. There is an old IBM story of a conversation between Tom Watson Sr. and one of his competitors. The latter commented, "Tom, it is hard times. I hear you are still hiring salesmen and I just can't see how that's a prudent thing for you to do."

Watson Sr. chuckled and replied, "Well, you know when a man gets to my age, he doesn't always do prudent things. Some men take to gambling, some men amass fortunes in art and some men hoard gold. Personally, I collect great salesmen."

Everyone at IBM was a salesman, and as Watson had come to believe, he was going to need each and every one of them.

The Great Depression

On October 30, 1929 — the day after Black Tuesday — Tom Watson Sr. stood before a room full of newly trained IBM salesmen. It was one of the darkest times in U.S. economic history. The *New York Times* had just written that the stock market suffered its "most disastrous" day in history, but Watson did not discuss the economy, cite a single financial statistic or mention the stock market. Instead he talked about democracy in business, pulling together as one man and the IBM Spirit. For the next four years he needed his team to do one thing: believe in one another.

Watson's team fought that economic beast successfully for more than three years. Dividends had been resumed in 1916, and it wasn't until January 1933 that this run fell into jeopardy — the internal financial forecast at that time was a year with "reduced or no dividends."[21] Unknown to the IBM team, they were forecasting the Great Depression's economic trough, which would come in March. It was an accurate financial forecast, and it looked as if the beast was going to finally best them.

If Watson had remained dogmatic in his perspective, he would have reverted to his 1914 philosophy and stopped dividend payments to ensure corporate survival. But it was a different time, a different set of circumstances, and because of 1921, he was a different man.

The IBM stockholder was also different—they were no longer of the elite. They were individuals of small means purchasing single shares to then buy food and shelter with the quarterly dividends. More than half of them (2,200 of 4,000 total stockholders) were women[22]—IBM had become a "widows and orphans" stock.

Since 1927, Watson had been telling his salesmen that these investments were not just in IBM, but in him and his team. It was not an option for them to throw up their hands—as they had in 1920—when business got bad. So in January 1933, Watson stood in front of his 1932 One Hundred Percent Club salesmen and told them that they had a great service to perform. Uncharacteristically, he invited non-Hundred Percenters, and to them he said bluntly, "Do something different." In his fourth morning session, he told his factory foremen, "You have to keep in mind that your duty is to those men [salesmen] out there." He instructed them to deliver higher quality products and to hire more men of character.

Watson was in overdrive. He needed his IBM team with him. So finally, possibly talking about himself as much as his team, he

Sailors are developed when the seas are rough.

told those who had been with him through the economic storms of the last nineteen years, "There never was a good sailor developed in fair weather. It is during the storms when the seas are running high and the going is rough that you develop your sailors. That is how you develop men."[23] He was determined to pay a dividend in 1933 and was calling on his team to help.

From *The World's Greatest Salesman*, provided by MBI Concepts Corp.

He promised to reward every IBMer's investment of time, dedication and loyalty, but he asked them to wait for better times. He would tell the entire IBM organization, "I am looking forward to an era, under the New Deal, in which we shall be able to pay everybody more money. I believe it is coming. But we have to build up to it."[24]

His team delivered. IBM paid its expected dividends and grew revenue, too. IBMers learned in the toughest of economic times to respect one another's words and hear the call of True Service. Respect was our cultural glue and Service defined our objectives. To Tom Watson Sr., Service was a fundamental belief: it stopped the pumping and dumping of IBM stock; it suppressed dividends to produce products with real customer value; and it prioritized widows and orphans over personal financial gain. Watson's concept of Service—giving beyond the thought of personal gain—called all employee-owners to a purpose greater than themselves. It created a corporate family unlike any of its day.

World War II

On December 8, 1941, the United States entered World War II, and Watson turned the full resources of IBM over to his government. He limited IBM's profits on the production of munitions to 1.5%—placing this amount in a fund for the widows and orphans of IBM war veterans—and he refused to profit personally from any business gains resulting from the war—retroactively reducing his 1941 earnings in 1942 (see Appendix F). It was now on Watson to model True Service, and that which he had said was coming—paying everybody more money—was on him to deliver.

In early 1942, after promising through the Depression that better times were ahead, he and the board of directors created the Watson Fund—a special reserve for subsidizing employee benefits. He bankrolled the fund by reducing his commission from 5% of profits left after payment of dividends to 2.5%. Then, after the war, he again reduced his commission—this time to just 0.5%:*

---

* Several authors have made much of Tom Watson Sr. being the "$1,000-a-day man" during the Great Depression. See Appendix F for insights on this topic.

> Thomas J. Watson, IBM president, cut his own pay in 1946 so that more than $500,000 could be added to the retirement fund for veteran IBM employees. Mr. Watson requested, and the IBM board of directors agreed, that his percentage compensation as specified in his employment contract for 1946 be reduced from 2½ per cent to a rate of one-half of 1 per cent. The board determined that this reduction amounted to $525,609.27. In accordance with Mr. Watson's request, directors added this amount to the **Watson Fund to supplement the IBM Retirement Plan**. The fund showed a balance of $1,912,083.94 at the end of 1946 after taking into account income from interest and expenditures in the form of benefit payments. [Emphasis added.][25]

These two voluntary reductions underwrote the beginning and ongoing improvements of the IBM Retirement Plan. Payments from the pension plan came from two sources: the IBM Retirement Plan itself and the Watson Fund for Supplementing the IBM Retirement Plan. At the inception of IBM's Retirement Plan in 1945, the Watson Fund paid 100% of the retirement plan's first year's pension payments.[26] Its share of these retirement payments would then gradually decline over the next eleven years to 20% by Watson's death in 1956 (see Appendix E).

When Watson died, his will provided for family, four organizations and forty-two employees (elevator operators, secretaries, receptionists and other past and present members of his personal staff). It was explained in his will that Mr. Watson was providing only for his immediate staff because "the Watson Fund provides benefit by way of increased retirement allowances for his other friends in the corporation."[27]

For four decades Watson was not only IBM's CEO but a fellow employee-owner. IBM's employee-owners stood by him in 1914 when the world believed he was a soon-to-be-imprisoned criminal, in 1921 when he lost sight of his most important asset, in the 1930s when he asked them to perform an act of True Service for the greater good, in 1942 when he refused to let his corporation profit from wartime munitions production, and over the rest of his four decades of leadership as he rebalanced the distribution of profits equitably between all his stakeholders.

He always believed we were at his side; he proved he was always at ours.

A Scaling Corporation

IBM's founder had discovered the best path for growth through the twentieth century. Unfortunately, he wasn't scalable. By the 1940s, all the needs of his corporation could no longer fit through his always open, but lone, door—now the thing that most inhibited his company's growth became the old man himself.

Watson Sr.'s nature was a personal one, but it could range from that of a father figure to that of a benevolent dictator. He was authoritarian, and his leadership style directly conflicted with the corporation he wanted to build—a society of thinking and acting individuals. And with all due respect to the fifty thousand IBMers of the time, IBM would have eventually died along with Watson if not for his son. Although by legal standards IBM was a corporation, it was still very much Watson Sr.'s personal property, and external forces were making internal change a necessity.

At the end of 1955 IBM employment stood at 56,000, net income at $56 million and revenue at $500 million. Rather than taking another four decades to match those numbers, Thomas J. Watson Jr. would add, on average, 56,000 employees every four years, $56 million in net income every nine months and $500 million in revenue almost every year. By 1971, revenue per employee had grown by 212%, net income per employee by 310% and the number of stockholders by more than 2,000%. Under his watch, IBM became the corporation his father had always envisioned.

How did he do this?

To start, Tom Watson Jr. kept his father's foundation but moved quickly to decentralize IBM and make the Basic Beliefs the common touchstone for evaluating, thinking and acting independently. He adhered to the same basic set of principles his father had developed to run the corporation, but his approach was a scalable one. He had inherited a company that was now famous for high pay, generous benefits and intense devotion "to Dad."[28] So Watson Jr. did not need to gain loyalty, he needed to shift it; and he transferred it to the corporation, not himself.

In 1956 Watson Jr. called a meeting in historic Williamsburg, Virginia—because it was meant to carry an aura of being a "constitutional convention"[29]—and initiated the building of his new IBM. In this meeting he delegated enormous power to his employee-owners and set up a system of checks and balances for control. He referred to it as IBM's Contention Management System.

The danger was that IBM could have ground to a halt in petty conflicts, but because Respect was still at the company's core—and the new CEO ruled within its constraints—IBM would grow exponentially.* This decentralized organization grew sales 34.8% the first year and between 12.6% and 21.2% each of the four years after that.[30] It also provided the management framework that delivered the System/360, taking Watson Jr.'s corporation from the back office of tabulators and typewriters to data centers full of mainframes.

Implementing the Basic Beliefs

Watson Sr. had communicated through maxims and speeches—topics included "Democracy in Business," "We Are All Assistants" and "We Forgive Thoughtful Mistakes"—and his employees communicated his beliefs through oral tradition. But as with any tradition, those beliefs would have eventually been extinguished or corrupted, which is why Watson Jr. summarized his father's principles, wrote them down and made everyone—including himself—subject to their rule. Through this, he decentralized an autocracy but controlled anarchy.

In Watson Sr.'s day, he was the enforcer—if management did something wrong, they feared his presence. In his son's day, everyone learned to respect the power of, consistency in and enforcement of IBM's Basic Beliefs. Individuals told how to think and act for so long were suddenly empowered to execute with a new freedom limited not by fear, but by

---

* Tom Watson Jr. highlighted other reasons: job security, high pay and stock options for his executives; individual accountability; and leaving himself free to roam the corporation. But I think he would agree that fundamentally, without employees having respect for one another, these other matters would have been moot. Since the foundation of Respect was already present, it did not warrant mentioning or need to be changed.

the constraints of an easily understood corporate constitution. Fifty-six thousand individuals were suddenly energized and put in motion.

Both Watsons understood that human beings wander. Again, Watson Sr. enforced his policies personally, but Watson Jr. put everything within the context of the Basic Beliefs. He initiated communication processes to flow information between himself and the individual employee-owner. To flow information up he initiated a Question and Answer Program, a Suggestion Award Program, Opinion Surveys (attitude surveys) and annual Employee Appraisals. To flow information down, Management Briefs informed managers of issues of concern; Executive Letters (President's Letters) went directly to those at the executive level; and Watson Jr. started publications at the plant, division and company levels. He continued IBM Family Days and made Open Doors and Executive Interviews—a two-way conduit of information—an expected norm of management at all levels, not just the corner office.

He articulated the reasoning behind these multiple processes in *A Business and Its Beliefs: The Ideas That Helped Build IBM*:

> You must make use of a number of pipelines, upward as well as downward. Parallel communication paths may seem unnecessary to some. But we have found that any single path can be only partly successful, that certain information flows better over some paths than others, and that all employees do not react in the same way to a given medium. Management must have a wide selection of communication means at its disposal. And, probably more important, the employee must have a variety of ways through which he can make his voice heard by management.[31]

Tom Watson Jr. also picked up his father's perspective on stockholders. He wrote in his IBM Management Principles (see Appendix G), an extension to the Basic Beliefs, that the company had an obligation to provide an *attractive* return on invested capital. "Attractive" is the most subjective of adjectives. It requires a courageous CEO to set shareholder expectations around such a word. What is an attractive return for shareholders? Watson Sr.'s actions, over his four decades, would seem to suggest his answer would have been, "It depends." Watson Jr.'s issuing of stock during his 1965 crisis—when IBM came within weeks of needing emergency loans to meet payroll—would suggest the same.

Over six decades, father and son faced twelve recessions and the Great Depression, each averaging fifteen months, and spanning four of the six largest stock market declines in history (see Appendix A). To guide their company, the Watsons constructed a corporate constitution—a guiding compass aligned to true north. No human institution will ever be perfect, but no matter how far we IBMers wandered, we always had the Watsons' compass and a heading set by these beliefs. Perfection may be unreachable, but during the journey, Respect for the Individual empowered us, controlled the power of the abusive and ensured right over might.

This was America's twentieth-century leadership at its best. The Watsons demanded that every employee be a salesman; they protected and invested in their most valuable asset; they thirsted to see through their employee-owners' eyes; they set a standard of True Service; and they built character to ensure right over might. This created a corporate culture, the strength of which few have comprehended, much less equaled.

This was the redwood forest I joined in 1980.

Endnotes

1 "Thomas John Watson 1874-1956 Memorial Issue," *THINK* (IBM), July, August, September 1956, p. 29.

2 The complete history of Tom Watson Sr. and NCR is well documented in Kevin Maney's *The Maverick and His Machine* (John Wiley and Sons, Inc., New York, 2003).

3 Thomas Graham Belden and Marva Robins Belden, *The Lengthening Shadow* (Little, Brown, Boston, 1962), p. 95.

4 Ibid., pp. 94, 95.

5 Peter E. Greulich, *The World's Greatest Salesman* (MBI Concepts Corporation, Austin, Texas, 2011), p. 32.

6 Ibid., p. 20.

7 William Inglis, *George F. Johnson and His Industrial Democracy* (Huntington Press, New York, 1935), pp. 35, 43.

8 Thomas Graham Belden and Marva Robins Belden, *The Lengthening Shadow* (Little, Brown, Boston, 1962), p. 100.

9 Ibid.

10 William Rogers, *THINK: A Biography of the Watsons and IBM* (Stein and Day, New York, 1969), p. 81.

11 © 2013 Morningstar. All rights reserved. *Morningstar 2013 Ibbotson SBBI Classic Yearbook* (Morningstar Inc., 2013), p. 160, used with permission.

12 Thomas Graham Belden and Marva Robins Belden, *The Lengthening Shadow* (Little, Brown, Boston, 1962), p. 116.

13 Kevin Maney, *The Maverick and His Machine* (John Wiley and Sons, Inc., New York, 2003), p. 87.

14 From personal interviews conducted by Peter E. Greulich, 2013.

15 "Computing-Tabulating Stock Sold," *Sun and the Globe*, June 27, 1923, p. 26.

16 Peter E. Greulich, *The World's Greatest Salesman* (MBI Concepts Corporation, Austin, Texas, 2011), p. 147.

17 Ibid., p. 10.

18 Peter E. Greulich, *Tom Watson Sr. Essays on Leadership, Volume III: We Forgive Thoughtful Mistakes* (MBI Concepts Corporation, Austin, Texas, 2012).

19 Peter E. Greulich, *The World's Greatest Salesman* (MBI Concepts Corporation, Austin, Texas, 2011), p. 147.

20 Peter E. Greulich, *Tom Watson Sr. Essays on Leadership, Volume III: We Forgive Thoughtful Mistakes* (MBI Concepts Corporation, Austin, Texas, 2012), p. 9.

21 Peter E. Greulich, *The World's Greatest Salesman* (MBI Concepts Corporation, Austin, Texas, 2011), p. 291.

22 Ibid., p. 104.

23 Ibid., p. 256.

24 Ibid., p. 278.

25 "Watson Cut Benefits Employee Fund," *Binghamton Press*, April 12, 1947, p. 3.

26 "New Retirement Plan Pays $60–$130 Monthly and Costs Million a Year," *Binghamton Press*, September 15, 1945.

27 "Four Organizations and 42 Employees Share in Watson Estate," *Binghamton Press*, July 20, 1956, p. 13.

28 Thomas J. Watson Jr., *Father, Son & Company* (Bantam Books, New York, 1990), p. 15.

29 Ibid., p. 285.

30 *Moody's Industrial Manual*, International Business Machines Corporation (Moody's, New York, 1966), p. 2842.

31 Thomas J. Watson Jr., *A Business and Its Beliefs* (McGraw-Hill Book Company, Inc., New York, Toronto, London, 1963), p. 60.

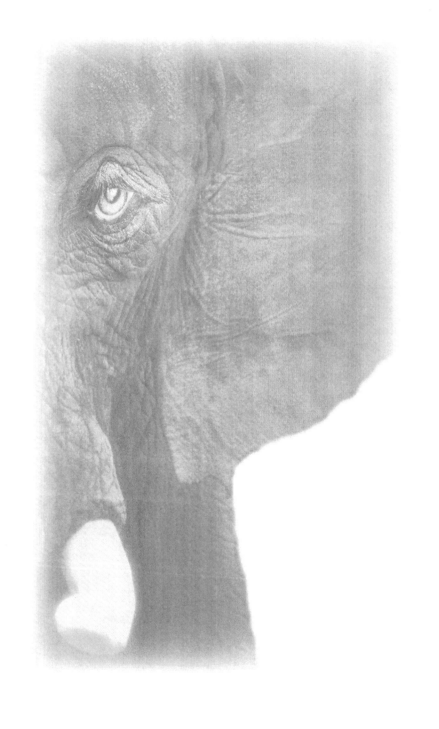

CHAPTER TWO

LIFE IN THE REDWOOD FOREST

> ❝ This business is different from others; this is not just an ordinary business. We speak of it as a great world institution. We are merely in it temporarily—just during the term of our lifetime—but the principles of this business are fixed. They are lasting principles."[1]
>
> **Thomas J. Watson Sr.**

Thoughtful Mistakes

> The pressure to perform in the organizations we will describe…is noth-
> ing short of brutal: these are "no excuse" environments, where radical
> decentralization frees people to make anything happen, where training
> is provided, where extraordinary results are then routinely expected be-
> cause the barriers to them have been removed…. They are both: tough
> on the values, tender in the support of people who would dare to take
> a risk and try something new in support of those values. They speak
> constantly of vision, of values, of integrity; they harbor the most soaring,
> lofty and abstract notions.[2]
>
> **Tom Peters and Nancy Austin**, *A Passion for Excellence*

When I joined IBM Austin in October 1980, Watson Sr. was a memory
and Watson Jr. had retired, but their belief system of Respect, Service
and Excellence roamed openly and freely. These principles entered every
room and bounded every discussion. Everyone watched out for them,
exercised them and cared intimately about them. IBM was tough on
these values. It was a "no excuse" environment.

At the time, computers were built to order and took months to ship.
Prior to the arrival of a computer, customers raised floors for electrical
wires, water pipes and extra cooling; upon arrival, the computer might
be dismantled and squeezed into an elevator or inserted by crane through
an upper-story window in a skyscraper. The delivery required advance
scheduling of hardware and software engineers to install the system and
get it into production. Demand was so high and the delay in shipping so
long that third party companies would place a positioning order during
a first-day order window and then sell that position in the queue to the
highest bidder. Imagine a customer queue wrapped around an Apple
store to obtain the latest iPhone—only it was for multimillion-dollar
computers. Fortunes were made selling a delivery date, and customers,
after doing the return-on-investment calculations, paid because the cost
of a two-month delay to their projects was even more.

To add extra stress, our sales branch had monthly, quarterly and end-
of-year sales targets, and only the successful installation of a computer

generated the necessary revenue to meet those goals. A month-end delay meant delayed commissions; miss the end of a quarter and large sales bonuses were jeopardized; miss a year-end installation and the entire office could be affected. So we accelerated many critical installations into that last twenty-four hours of a month, quarter or (worst from a stress standpoint) year.

The sales reps understood their customers' industries and long-term goals. They managed the IBM-to-customer relationship, while administration managed all other details. It was my job to coordinate the pricing, configuring, ordering, scheduling, transportation, installation and billing for these computers. We did this work to keep the IBM salesmen focused on one goal: closing deals. Distractions from selling were not allowed.

Within weeks of joining IBM, I made a mistake that delayed the installation of a major computer upgrade. It cost the customer time and money. Although it was not at a quarter or year end, it was at a month end, and it delayed the sales rep's commission check. My manager, Tom, who had hired me not a month earlier, called me into his office.

As I walked in, he rolled back in his chair and pointed at the door for me to close it.

He went right to it: "Pete, what went wrong?"

I went into a lengthy explanation. I knew that I was responsible. I fully accepted that. Others had failed to deliver critical information that I needed, but I owned asking the right questions.

Since Tom had hired me, I felt I had let him down. I wondered if he was questioning his decision. After I was done, he paused, looked at me and started slowly into a story I would hear many times at IBM:

"I think it was the 1940s. IBM had survived the Great Depression, and World War II had just ended. IBM war veterans were returning home to claim their former jobs. Tom Watson Sr. had limited profits from war production, but to maintain full employment he kept the manufacturing lines running. He was filling warehouses all over the country with inventory when there was little demand. He was gambling on a postwar boom. With the war ending, he needed these inventories sold. A large government deal worth over a million dollars came through the door, and of course, Watson was personally involved.

"The IBM Corporation—actually no, the old man—needed this deal, but the sales rep failed and IBM lost to a competitor.

"The sales rep showed up that day to give Mr. Watson the news. He outlined each step of the deal, highlighted where mistakes had been made and what could have been done differently." Tom leaned forward, made eye contact with me and nodded. "Probably just like you did today.

"Finally the sales representative stood up and said, 'Thank you, Mr. Watson, for giving me a chance to explain. I know we needed this deal. I know what it meant to you.' And he rested his resignation on the CEO's desk."

I was in shock. I knew the late delivery had cost the customer time and money, that they were not happy, and that the sales representative was mad beyond belief, but was this enough for IBM to fire me? I wondered if I should have come into the office with *my* resignation in hand.

"That IBM sales representative moved to leave, but the old man

Respect makes tough conversations possible and productive.

met him at the door. He handed the envelope back, saying, 'Why would I accept this resignation when I have just invested a million dollars in your education?' "

I am sure my eyes watered up. Tom chuckled with satisfaction.

He smiled. "Pete, IBM spent a few dollars on your education this week. Learn from it. We expect the best in everything you do, especially when customer satisfaction, revenue recognition and timely payment of commissions are at risk."

I got up to leave, but Tom met me at his office door and held it closed. He said, "Pete, if the sales representative gives you a hard time over this,

I want to know. As far as IBM is concerned, this has been handled. It is my opinion that you have just made a thoughtful mistake."

Eliminating the Elephant in the Room

Over the years, I have often thought of that day. I believe Tom was more pleased with his delivery of the story than anything else. I would hear this story used in sales meetings, plant gatherings and administrative assemblies. Although the form of the story changed and the forgiven character was adapted to the audience, there was always one consistent message: IBM forgives thoughtful mistakes. In 1934, Watson Sr. had said:

> If a man thinks about his work—if he puts real thought into everything he does, he should be and *will be* forgiven for the mistakes he makes. I do not believe in criticizing a man simply for making a mistake. If he shows that he has given the proper amount of thought to a matter; if he shows that he has tried to do the right thing; I am ready to forgive thoughtful mistakes.[3]

The million-dollar mistake happened some twelve years later. As a percentage of IBM's net income, it was the equivalent of forgiving a $1.5 billion mistake today. But Watson needed his corporation to grow, and to accomplish that he needed independent thought and action. So he invested in a simple story as surely as he would have a piece of machinery. He always expected a return on his investments, and this one achieved more than four decades of returns. It lived so strongly that thirty-four years later it transformed two employees from manager and employee into two men who respected each other.

Wherever important matters are discussed, there are elephants in the room: fail to acknowledge their presence and results become unpredictable as unacknowledged motives take control. But the Watsons demanded predictability, so they made the IBM Basic Beliefs their surrogates in every room, every discussion and every decision. This one story was just a single example of the many oral traditions they designed to illuminate and eliminate elephants.

If an employee displayed consistent carelessness, showed an uncaring attitude or made thoughtless mistakes, he or she would be fired. But Tom, as my first-line administration manager, spoke with the delegated authority of a CEO. There was no need for anyone else in his office that day but us and the Basic Beliefs. Respect demanded that he discuss my performance with me, make Service to the customer our common objective and Excellence — not necessarily found in the first few weeks on the job — the pursued path. Each case like mine was handled on its own merits, and Tom was empowered to make a decision.

Where these beliefs lived, there was no room for an elephant.

Building Commitment

Some people who start out in modest circumstances have a certain contempt for the average man when they are able to rise above him. Others, by the time they become leaders, have built up a unique respect and understanding for the average man and a sympathy for his problems. They recognize that in a modern industrial nation the less fortunate often are victims of forces not wholly within their own control. T. J. Watson [Sr.] was in the latter category. He had known hard times, hard work, and unemployment himself, and he always had understanding for the problems of the working man. Moreover, he recognized that the greatest of these problems was job security.[4]

Thomas J. Watson Jr., *A Business and Its Beliefs*

John Opel, who took over for Frank Cary as IBM's CEO in 1981, launched a tremendous investment spree. We were going to be a $100 billion corporation by 1990. Even though the U.S. economy was just entering what would be a sixteen-month-long recession that wouldn't find bottom until November 1982, we spent money expecting to reach that goal. We built factories, and between 1980 and 1985 we hired sixty thousand people.

In capitalism, a for-profit business is an especially hard place to manage employees when a growth expectation faces recessionary headwinds. But it was against this backdrop that I experienced the determination and strength of a corporate family culture.

A little more than two years into my job, I would check "single, head of household" instead of "married, filing jointly" on my tax return. I was now economically and emotionally responsible for two daughters ages six and one and a son age three. As if the emotional responsibility wasn't enough, I quickly realized that an IBM administrator's pay was not going to be sufficient. I would find day care for my two youngest and after-school care for my oldest, only to realize that when school let out, the cost of summer care for all three would consume my entire paycheck. To start saving, I called the mortgage company to arrange interest-only payments on my mobile home loan. But the economic strains weren't just coming next summer, they were already here, at the weekly grocery checkout—so, as many do during difficult times, I floated today's personal check against tomorrow's paycheck. Then it was a lunchtime race to beat the grocer to my bank.

In 1982 there were no home offices. Administrative work, especially, was performed at the place of employment: answer the phone; perform data entry; read, shuffle and store papers in manila folders in filing cabinets. If you weren't at work, you weren't producing, and the business suffered. As I struggled with the devolution from orderly two-parent household to single-parent chaos, my performance became erratic. There were the absences from work, avoiding of overtime, sickness from stress, hair lice, low-grade fevers, parent-teacher conferences, early morning drop-offs and after school pickups. One day, as I loaded my children into the car, the day-care instructor commented, "I know your work number by heart." That pretty much summed up my life.

I thought I could keep it under control, but eventually I realized I had to bring Tom into the equation.

He got right to the point: "Pete, I knew something was wrong. Your performance has dropped, but your personal life is your personal life until you tell me otherwise. Are you telling me otherwise?"

I looked out the window. There was an elephant in the room I was afraid of mentioning. "Tom, I'm not sure I can make it as a single parent."

"Do you mean financially or personally?"

"Both," I said.

He paused for a moment, because he was about to violate corporate policy. "You have a pay raise coming in a few months and it is substantial. I have also put you in for an award that should go through. So in a few months you will be on much better financial footing. We all know that the IBM Austin administrative salaries are the lowest in the country, and I have been working hard to compensate for it. But there is only so much I can do in a short period of time." He almost sounded apologetic.

"Tom, I—"

"You can't tell anyone what I just told you," he interrupted. "If for some reason the pay raise doesn't come through on time, you have to be patient. And no award is guaranteed until it is put in your hands. I know you won't tell anyone about this, or you're a dead man, right?"

I just nodded. I always had trouble expressing gratitude. It would eventually get said, but I always had to compose myself first, and usually it would be done in writing.

Tom did what he could for me financially: the award came and the raise arrived on time. Emotionally, though, the fear of losing my job was an elephant that just wouldn't go away: it tapped on my shoulder at 5:15 when I left unfinished work to get to the day care before closing; it wrapped its trunk tightly around my chest with each new childhood sickness; in my nightmares it answered the phone and placed it against my ear so Tom could say, "Pete, we need to talk."

Ear infections for my youngest became a vicious circle. Mornings started with her tugging at her ear. With fingers crossed, I checked her temperature. Then off to day care hoping she would make it through the day. But the call would always come. Then take off work, pick her up, take her to the doctor, write a check for amoxicillin, head back to the same day care to pick up her brother, gather up her sister from after-school care, cook dinner and finally rock the youngest to sleep. And my personal, ever-present elephant valet gently pushed the rocking chair with its trunk. A week later it would start all over again.

I begged our doctor to put tubes in her ears—I couldn't afford to be out of work anymore. He told me to wait "just a bit longer." He had become a good friend, and he knew I couldn't afford the operation.

"A little longer and I will be out of work," I told him.

The elephant grimaced. It prefers anonymity.

But it would be her last ear infection. I found work-arounds for everything but illness, and that became less frequent. Life settled down. I was almost in the clear.

Then one morning, after waking up my eldest daughter, I found her covered in sores.

I usually cried in private, but there was no stopping it at that moment.

"Daddy, what's wrong?" she asked.

"Chicken pox." I choked on the words. "I'll be out of work for two weeks." How could I call Tom again? And I could see another four weeks following her, as my two youngest looked curiously at her sores.

And how the elephant danced!

Fortunately, the chicken pox party I threw that night concentrated the two next cases into one. I would *only* be out for four weeks instead of six. Tom, with each daily call, reassured me; Gene and Sandra picked up my workload; even the sales reps asked what they could do. One invited me to Thanksgiving dinner. When he found out the situation, he commented, "I can't remember if I've had chicken pox. I'd better call home."

Tom proved to me that he always had my back. My IBM family stayed with me. They pulled harder to minimize the impact on both me and IBM. And when I returned, I worked harder than ever to return their commitment to me. The way to do that was to make IBM successful, to keep us profitable, and to live the value system I was thriving in. We lived in a Watson IBM, and it built commitment to the corporation by supporting the individual. It took a long time, but IBM rid me of my very personal elephant—fear of homelessness.

Thirty years later, I took Gene—the senior administrator at the time—to lunch and we reminisced about these times. I told him what I'd gone through and thanked him for picking up the additional workload. He just shrugged his shoulders and said, "Pete, I don't even remember. You know, we all just did what needed to be done."

Our commitment was to one another, and together we were IBM.

Building Family

> You don't understand. I want them [managers] to be educated in *IBM* management: communications, supreme sales and service efforts, going to a guy's house if his wife is ill and seeing if you can help out, making post-death calls.[5]
>
> **Thomas J. Watson Jr.,** *Father, Son & Company*

Death had missed me for the first thirty years of my life. I had never come face-to-face with the loss of a family member or even a close acquaintance. The first time it found me, it was my IBM family that would feel the impact.

Although Tom and I were still manager and employee, we became friends. I had proven myself worthy of the title of IBMer, and he had earned my trust and confidence, not so much as a manager, but at a deeper level as a mentor and confidant. He was a person who knew how to balance business and personal life, and he laughed, joked and made the office a place you wanted to be.

One day the Austin branch office team went on one of our numerous family outings. IBM rented a houseboat and anchored it in the middle of Lake Travis. We laughed, danced and dove from the houseboat's second-floor platform. We worked hard, but we also played hard, as the trademark IBM wingtip shoes, white shirts and ties came off. The lake was about T-shirts, shorts and family. We bathed under the Texas sun all day.

As we packed to leave, we all had sunburns, but Tom had a particularly bad one.

Cancer.

I don't remember much about that time. I was still a single parent with three children so there wasn't much I could do. I provided moral support, and as others had done for me, I took on more responsibilities at work, picking up the slack during Tom's physical and emotional absences. His hair fell out. The laughter stopped.

The cancer did go into remission. His hair grew back, and the laughter returned. But not for long. It was only a short time later that I was sitting in Tom's office, just visiting and discussing business, when he looked at me and said, "Pete, it's back."

I knew instantly what he meant. I looked into his eyes to see what was going to come next. Usually I could tell what he was thinking—we had worked together for years—but there was no reading him that day. He just looked so tired.

"I just don't have the strength to go through this again." He swallowed hard.

Death reached into the room and, in my presence, touched a fellow IBMer and dear friend.

Tom had always been there to check on my mistakes. He had rejoiced in my ongoing success. He had brought me up in IBM. He was grooming me for first-line management. And within weeks death took him, and for the first time in my life I had to grapple with the loss of a friend.

The IBM Austin office closed for his funeral. The entire sales branch of more than one hundred people was there. There were no words in me that day. The sorrow was too deep. I could not have spoken if I'd wanted to. Deep regrets were just below the surface, and I didn't want anyone to scratch that surface or I would have cried uncontrollably.

All relationships have rocky times. Tom and I, as in any family, had our tough moments and sticky conversations. That day I regretted every cross word I had ever said. I regretted the last moments I spent speechless at the foot of his hospital bed, when we all knew the end was near. I regretted that I hadn't found the voice to tell him how much he had meant to my family; tell him he had made a difference in this world; tell him my children would always owe him a now unpayable debt for our financial stability. Because of him, they would grow up with a roof over their heads. I knew that I had earned it, but he exercised that power given to him to deliver security when I needed it the most. With some other company or some other management style, it could have easily been different. With another company or another manager that didn't exercise the power given them, we would have been on the street. I promised myself that day never again to let such words go unsaid.

The funeral was scary for me, a morose event that I didn't understand. Its importance was hidden behind a veil of uncertainty as to what to say and a fear of saying the wrong thing. This was the day I first understood that funerals are for the living.

Tom's eight-year-old son stood in front of me. I stood silently, stoically,

We were family.

watching and thinking of my own children. I wondered if any child could ever understand what was happening. Then Tom's son moved closer to his mother. He lifted up his arm and pointed to Bill, Tom's manager—my second-line manager—across the way.

He said, "See that man over there. He flew all the way from Atlanta to be here!"

He paused for a moment, watching Bill, trying to comprehend what was going on. Then he dropped his head, and under his breath said, "My dad was a *really important man.*"

"He surely was," I whispered to myself.

A veil was lifted.

Expectations of IBM's Twentieth-Century Management

That day, in the then-small, remote town of Austin, Texas, our managers personified the IBM spirit. Bill modeled his foremost job for all of us. It had always been Tom's. From that day forward I would always try to make it mine. Yearly pay raises, profit sharing and stock options, when put into perspective, would never again seem quite as important.

I wanted to be a manager for this company more than anything else in the world. It was a sad day when IBM lost a good manager, a good father, a good friend and a good man. Tom left in me a great desire to follow in his footsteps as an IBM manager.

"You can pay me no greater compliment," I think, would have been his words.

Building Excellence

> Let us make self-analysis a habit and teach the habit down the line to all the other men. Putting himself through a mental sorting, a tabulating machine as it were, is the only process whereby a man can accomplish the difficult and highly important task of knowing himself.[6]
>
> **Thomas Watson Sr.**

Within two years of Tom's death, I achieved my goal: I was promoted to first-line administration manager.

A few months later, still wet behind the ears, my branch office held its yearly Opinion Survey, in which the employees evaluated everything about the company—with an entire section focused on their immediate manager. Each Opinion Survey was followed by an as-long-as-it-takes feedback session. In this session, that manager would go through every survey question as completely as the team wanted. If the manager sensed hesitation, they dug deeper. It was a time of openness and honesty—flowing from the employees to the manager. IBM's management was expected to be the best in the industry, and this was every manager's most grueling yearly examination.

And for the first time, instead of evaluating, I was being evaluated.

The 1985 Opinion Survey was approximately one hundred questions with ratings ranging from 1 to 5. A 1 was best and a 5 terrible. Our branch leader, my third-line manager, discouraged anyone from checking a 3. She told our teams to "Take a stand. When in doubt, check a 2 or a 4. Give us something to work with, not a shrug of the shoulders."

Gary, my manager, saw my results first. He needed to prepare me for my first feedback session.

"Pete, your team gave you a three," Gary said, "a shoulder shrug."

I thought, "Well, I have only been in the job for a few months, so I can build on that."

But Gary confronted those thoughts: "Pete, this is a middle-of-the-road evaluation. It is critical we fix it." He focused his eyes on mine. "Your Opinion Survey wasn't bad, but it wasn't good. You need to discover what it is that you need to change."

Shaking my head, I questioned him. "Change what?"

"I can't answer that for you," he said. "You need to change something about yourself and your management style. I don't know what it is, but your team does. You really need to talk to your people." Gary always walked this fine line between gravity and assurance. "We aren't going to fire you, but you will be removed from IBM management if your team says you are still a 3 a year from now. Listen to them in your feedback session. Be completely and thoroughly prepared."

I realized that I was under an unusual magnifying glass. I was used to being inspected by my boss, but this time it was my team holding the optics. In this feedback session they were going to be my superiors. Among them would be employees I had given good and bad appraisals; employees I had awarded generous and not so generous raises; and one I was sure shouldn't be an IBM employee at all. My management dream was hanging by a thread, and IBM had given my team a pair of scissors.

"From what I can tell," Gary continued, "there is a pattern to some of the write-in comments. They seem to suggest that you get defensive when challenged."

"You *damn* well don't say?"

We both laughed. "Heard it before?" he said.

"You know I have."

He knew because he had told me as much a few months earlier. He wasn't going to wait six months for Opinion Survey results, so he had conducted Executive Interviews (EIs) with members of my team. In these EIs this particular topic had surfaced with several team members.

"Pete, you will do okay," he said, reassuring me. "You know that I have been checking on you. Ask a lot of questions. Anytime you are under stress, ask questions and ask them to elaborate. When you feel yourself wanting to pontificate, take a deep breath and ask more questions."

"So I pontificate now?"

"Well that was one of the write-ins," he said. "Since I heard it in one of my EIs, I know it is meant in serious jest. Pete, I also know your team wants you to succeed. Ask them why they feel the way they do; ask them what you do that gives them the impression you are defensive; ask them for specific examples. Don't

Elephants were not allowed in an opinion survey feedback session.

let them shrug their shoulders like they did in the survey. Don't stop until you have concrete examples of what they see, hear and feel. My sense is that you have a good relationship with them. Rely on it to get out of them what you need."

He switched to encouragement mode. "It isn't a bad survey. If it were, I would be doing the feedback session, not you. Just study the results, prepare your thoughts, and when in doubt—"

"Ask more questions. I've got it."

"Do not let them off the hook. Keep digging. Your job depends on it."

Several individuals on my team had worked at IBM longer than I had been alive. They had seen IBM managers come and go, and because of their dedication and commitment many a young manager had been promoted on their watch. So when I walked into the room, I was more nervous than I had ever been; and although I had read everything IBM provided on conducting a proper feedback session, it was on me to make it successful, and I wasn't even sure how to define that success. But I figured I would recognize it if I tripped over it.

I turned on the foil projector. It was one of the loudest clicks I had ever heard in my life. As the fan blew heat in my face, I thought, "It's going to be a long day."

I put a foil on the overhead and asked the first question: "How would you rate IBM as a company to work for, compared with other companies you know about?"

It was a short conversation — 100% satisfied and favorable.

Then I broke all the rules and turned off the overhead. Looking at Charlie, one of the Quarter Century Club members in the room, I asked, "Charlie, Gary told me to start with an easy question. Okay, I've done that. Now let's get to what I need to know. What do I need to change most to be a better manager?"

Charlie leaned back in his chair and, as usual, gave it to me straight: "Pete, you do a great job getting our opinion. You talk to everyone. You explain your views and you do take the time to get the information you need."

"Charlie, enough of the touchy, feely stuff."

"*Make a decision*," he said. "That is your job. It comes with the territory. You seem to ponder everything. We know you own the final decision and will suffer the consequences if it is wrong. You seem to be afraid that we won't like it. What we dislike most is indecision. It's keeping us from getting our jobs done."

I looked around the room and everyone nodded in agreement.

I chuckled as I realized that Charlie had done his homework, too. He was prepared to tell me what he thought. He had his mental list and was ready to go through it. For six months he had been observing me, and now I had the opportunity to hear his thoughts. What I had feared most in my session was silence, and Charlie started the flow of words. I now understood why the Watsons spent so much time with their long-service employee-owners.

"Do you care to comment on my defensiveness?" I asked. "Gary said it is a common thread in the write-in comments and from his EIs."

"Well, you seem to have handled that well enough. We may keep you around for another year if—"

"I don't pontificate anymore?"

The room broke out in laughter. Having been in my team's shoes, I knew that a manager's strengths and weaknesses were constant lunch chatter, so, as I had suspected, the word "pontificate" was well known. We were on our way to a productive meeting.

I spent the rest of the day standing in front of my team dissecting those one hundred questions. Gary, Charlie and my teammates guided me to the finish line. IBM had put success in front of me to trip over. I instructed my team to start giving me a decision-by date, and I started making decisions.

When the 1986 Opinion Survey arrived, Gary had moved on to another job, but I knew what I had needed to do, and hopefully I had done it. The results from this second survey rested on my desk. I took a deep breath, exhaled and reached for the package. I opened it and immediately reviewed the "golden five questions"—the ones that would determine my management fate.

1. How good a job do you feel is being done by your immediate manager?
   100% favorable

2. How would you rate your immediate manager in terms of ability to manage business/technical responsibilities?
   100% favorable

3. How would you rate your immediate manager in terms of ability to manage people responsibilities?
   92% favorable

4. There is effective two-way communication between me and my manager.
   92% favorable

5. How much trust and confidence do you have in your immediate manager?
   100% favorable[7]

There was no shoulder shrug this year, and there was one write-in comment that I particularly enjoyed: "The pontification has stopped, thank you!"

Ensuring Right over Might

IBM made me not just a better manager, but a better person. Whether it was an Open Door, a Speak Up!, an Executive Interview or an Opinion Survey, the twentieth-century IBM processes were in place to protect what the Watsons considered a very real corporate concern—ensuring right over might. As Watson Sr. said:

> To establish sales morale, it is essential to start building at the top of the organization. The old idea that those in administrative positions should be autocrats has gone. The day of the section boss in business has passed. Every manager in every department of business, in factory, office or field, should remember that his duty is to help the men under his direction.[8]

Watson Jr. echoed those thoughts:

> I'm sure that a policy of this kind [Open Doors] makes many a traditional manager's blood run cold. He probably sees it as a challenge to his authority or, worse yet, as a sharp sword hanging over his head. But the fact remains that in IBM it has been remarkably effective, primarily because—by its mere existence—it exercises a moderating influence on management. Whenever a manager makes a decision affecting one of his people, he knows that he may be held accountable to higher management for the fairness of that decision.[9]

An Opinion Survey guaranteed an IBM manager a very personal self-analysis at least once a year. It ensured that IBM's leaders were strong and powerful yet coachable; the rest were returned to non-management positions. It was trust and confidence in reverse—from IBM's twentieth-century leadership, down.

This 1986 Opinion Survey was the last in our division, and possibly the last meaningful one in the company. IBM's new leadership was gradually removing the Watson management filters. The moderating influences on management power slowly disappeared. IBM stopped investing in making managers better human beings, and autocrats infiltrated the company. By 1988, I was questioning my trust and confidence in IBM's new leadership. I would often wonder why my company was morphing into something that at times was almost unrecognizable.

The answer arrived on a bright, sunny Austin day as I picked up my phone and heard, "This is the CEO's office, John Akers' administrative assistant speaking. I am calling about your Speak Up!"

Endnotes

1 Peter E. Greulich, *The World's Greatest Salesman* (MBI Concepts Corporation, Austin, Texas, 2011), p. 145.

2 Tom Peters and Nancy Austin, *A Passion for Excellence* (Random House, New York, 1985), p. xix.

3 Thomas J. Watson Sr., *Men—Minutes—Money* (IBM Corporation, New York, 1934), p. 325, reprinted with permission of IBM.

4 Thomas J. Watson Jr., *A Business and Its Beliefs* (McGraw-Hill Book Company, Inc., New York, Toronto, London, 1963), p. 14.

5 Thomas J. Watson Jr., *Father, Son & Company* (Bantam Books, New York, 1990), p. 303.

6 Thomas J. Watson Sr., *Men—Minutes—Money* (IBM Corporation, New York, 1934), p. 52, reprinted with permission of IBM.

7 IBM, Peter E. Greulich's 1986 IBM Opinion Survey Feedback Results, questions 41–45.

8 Peter E. Greulich, *The World's Greatest Salesman* (MBI Concepts Corporation, Austin, Texas, 2011), p. 26.

9 Thomas J. Watson Jr., *A Business and Its Beliefs* (McGraw-Hill Book Company, Inc., New York, Toronto, London, 1963), p. 20.

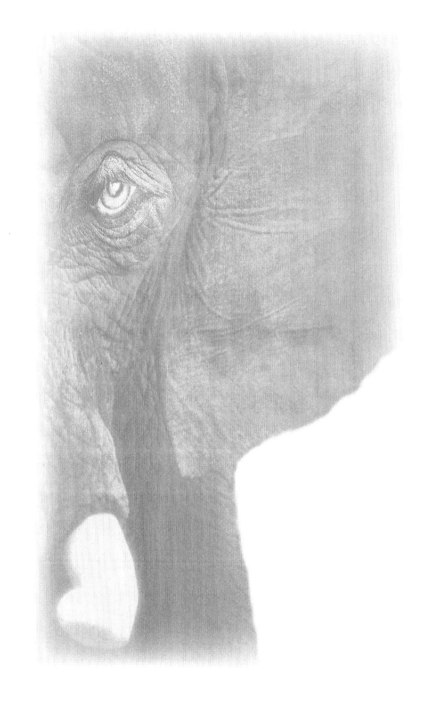

CHAPTER THREE

A CULTURE UNDER PRESSURE

> ❝ I have often told you that we want your suggestions and criticisms. I sometimes think you do not criticize us enough. Perhaps it is because you think so much of your associates at 50 Broad Street [IBM Headquarters in New York City] that you do not feel you should be critical, but when we do the wrong thing it is our friends who criticize us and our enemies who tell us we are right."[1]
>
> **Thomas J. Watson Sr.**, *Men — Minutes — Money*

> ❝ You don't hear things that are bad about your company unless you ask. It is easy to hear good tidings, but you have to scratch to get the bad news."[2]
>
> **Thomas J. Watson Jr.**, *Father, Son & Company*

IBM Stumbles Entering the 1990s

The cover story of *BusinessWeek* on February 18, 1985, was called "IBM: More Worlds to Conquer." The caption on the cover read: "It bets on software and communications to quadruple revenue by 1994."

The article inside boasted of IBM's tremendous success in previous years:

> Overall, the company has never been stronger. Assets at year end were about $40 billion. Net earnings in 1984 rose nearly 20%, to $6.6 billion—more than the total sales of its nearest competitor, DEC. Revenue grew about 14% despite a strong dollar that depressed overseas results. Had growth been measured in local currencies, IBM's worldwide revenue gain would have been near 19%....

> For sheer hubris, its schedule for growth has no par. Barring global economic crisis, the company plans to more than double its revenues, to $100 billion annually, by 1990. By 1994, revenues should nearly double again, to at least $185 billion.... In a watershed strategic statement four years ago, Chairman John R. Opel, then CEO, decreed that IBM should match or beat the information processing industry's growth in all segments—increases that range from up to 12% per year for large mainframe computers to 40% for personal computers and software.[3]

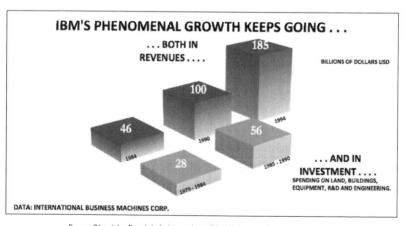

From: Chart by Derrick A. Langshaw/BW, Photograph by Doug Fowley

Setting an Unachievable Market Expectation

Unachievable expectations are a salesman's worst enemy, and Opel had just set an expectation that IBM would grow by more than 16% per year for nine straight years. A cursory look at the previous years' growth might have led him to think this was achievable—gains of 14.3%, 16.9%, 18.2%, 10.9% and 14.6%, respectively. Unfortunately, as we will see, those numbers were based on a financial game and net earnings would soon plummet. The actual revenue growth rates in the following three years were 8.9%, 2.4% and 5.8%. IBM's market expectations, it would seem, *were* set in hubris.

During the sales process, the sales representative controls customer expectations or suffers the consequences. We communicate and control expectations hundreds of times a year. In critical situations we will work and rework, adjust and readjust, align and realign our customer and corporation expectations to maintain a win-win relationship.

Similarly, John Opel's first job as IBM's salesman-in-chief should have been to establish and control market expectations. He set the expectation that IBM would be a $100 billion corporation by fiscal year 1990, which reflected the intuition of a person with a sales background. Revenue growth is hard, but it is the path chosen through sales initiative. In sales, you drive customer satisfaction. You position the right product with the right features at the right price at the right time in the right channels. You humble the competition. You monetize your product.

Unfortunately, $100 billion, much less $185 billion, would prove unachievable. While revenue grew over the next six years by more than 50%, IBM would ultimately miss Opel's market expectation by more than 30%—some $30 billion. Its net earnings would initially fall and then fluctuate to remain flat after six years of growth. (See Fig. 1, p. 58)

Big Blue was in trouble. Not since 1921 had such an error of judgment been made. Because of these mistakes we would slide to a revenue bottom of $62.7 billion, lose more than $8 billion in a single year, and one out of every two full-time IBMers would be ushered out of the business.

Our CEO needed to rework everyone's expectations. Instead, he left the expectations to his heir.

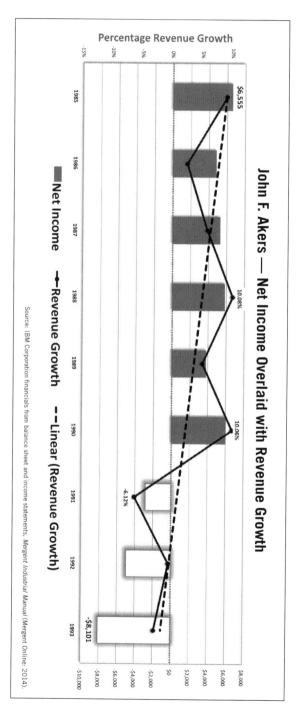

Fig.1 John F. Akers — Net Income Overlaid with Revenue Growth

In a corporate behemoth it may take years to reveal the full impact of an executive's decision, or a sharp economic downturn may expose it overnight. John Akers was holding the bag when both combined to demolish the drive to the $100 billion mark. He inherited an employment tsunami.

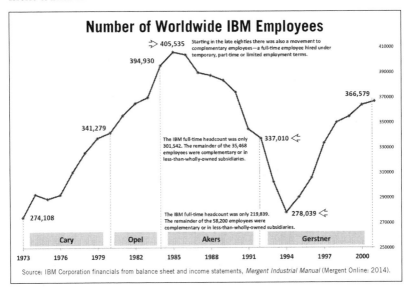

Number of Worldwide IBM Employees

Starting in the late eighties there was also a movement to complementary employees—a full-time employee hired under temporary, part-time or limited employment terms.

The IBM full-time headcount was only 301,542. The remainder of the 35,468 employees were complementary or in less-than-wholly-owned subsidiaries.

The IBM full-time headcount was only 219,839. The remainder of the 58,200 employees were complementary or in less-than-wholly-owned subsidiaries.

405,535
394,930
341,279
337,010
278,039
274,108
366,579

Cary   Opel   Akers   Gerstner

1973   1976   1979   1982   1985   1988   1991   1994   1997   2000

Source: IBM Corporation financials from balance sheet and income statements, *Mergent Industrial Manual* (Mergent Online: 2014).

In his first year, the hiring momentum would carry IBM to an employment peak of 405,535. He had to stop the ramp-up and then implement reductions. By the end of 1992, he had cut the IBM workforce by 17%, to 337,010. With the additional shift to complementary employees,* he reduced the IBM full-time workforce by 26%, to 301,542—one out of every four full-time IBMers was now gone. In the midst of these actions the U.S. stock market crumpled in a short but disastrous downturn, plummeting 30% from August 1987 to the end of that year. Morningstar's 2013 Ibbotson Stocks, Bonds, Bills, and Inflation (SBBI) Classic Yearbook lists this drop as the tenth largest decline in U.S. stock market history.[4] The internal damage was extensive. From 1991 to 1993, IBM would lose a total of $15.9 billion.

---

* From IBM annual reports: a complementary workforce is "an approximation of equivalent full-time employees hired under temporary, part-time and limited term employment arrangements to meet specific business needs in a flexible and cost-effective manner."

In a cruel twist of fate, John Akers' time ran out just as the U.S. stock market started one of the greatest bull runs in history. In less than two years, IBM was hiring again; but it would take almost two decades to achieve $100 billion. This surely left an indelible impression on any of John Akers' administrative assistants: meeting revenue growth expectations is hard. What they should have learned was that unrealistic market expectations can ruin a corporation's credibility and destroy it financially.

Depleting a Valuable Resource

I was in branch office administration from 1980 until late 1986. At that time the majority of IBM's revenue stream came from renting or leasing its equipment. Selling off this hardware base would be a fast way to generate revenue, and IBM decided this was the path to take. We prepared the customer contracts to convert their lease equipment to purchase. IBM sales reps, who were used to hard sales, did not find one here. The lease-to-purchase conversion could have demanded a premium dollar, but sales reps told us, "This is a no-brainer. The return on investment is so short that all I have to do is put this paperwork in front of the customer." It was a fire sale. We spiked revenue by exchanging an annual one-dollar gold piece for a one-time, devalued two-dollar paper note.

In the drive to become the Hundred Billion Dollar IBM, our revenue growth—already spectacular by any business standard—flared and exploded from its nitro-fueled injection. We invested in machinery, people and factories. By 1988 IBM's lease revenue—which in 1979 was 60% of our yearly income and had grown an average of 10.4% per year for the previous eight years—was surgically scalpeled from annual reports to fund this growth. (See Fig. 2, p. 61)

In the sales branch offices we couldn't see that the blaze was about to consume us. We were depleting a valuable, stable and growing lease revenue stream. To compensate, without a corresponding increase in territory or product coverage, annual quotas were doubled and tripled while product prices were in a free fall. A perfect storm had engulfed the IBM sales branch offices.

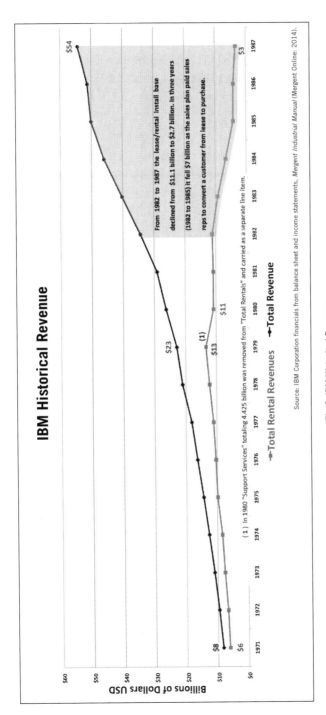

Fig.2 IBM Historical Revenue

Failing to See Through Their Salesmen's Eyes

The IBM sales force was caught in a corporate-generated sales stagflation. To compensate for the lost lease revenue, quotas were **inflated** year-over-year by 100% to 200% even as the price of computing power **deflated**. Over the next few years a $50,000 AS/400 would become sufficient to handle the workload of what had once cost three times that. We wondered aloud how IBM would cover our commission checks.

The business model was broken. Our billing systems were broken. Our partner support broke. Our internal organizations constantly reorganized. Our best and brightest were given incentives to retire and work elsewhere—two years' pay, bonuses, bridges to retirement and medical. Our leader was on a mission to break us up into baby blues—small, independent companies. As a corporation we were self-destructing; but in the sales branch office, where we owned the customer relationship, we refused to give up. We continued to put the customer first, determined to hold the line.

I would think of Tom often in those years, because ultimately it was about ownership, and more than any employee in corporate history, IBMers were employee-owners—individuals invested in their customers, their company and their company's stock. In the eighties, IBM sales reps would bounce into the office waving a contract and saying, "Closed a big deal today. Let's get that stock price up."

The first time I realized how dependent the individual IBMer was on our corporate success was Monday, October 19, 1987—commonly referred to as Black Monday. If you worked for IBM at the time, you probably remember where you were. I was one of more than twelve thousand IBMers being redeployed to direct customer support roles in a "back to the field" movement. In the middle of a sales training class in Atlanta, someone opened the door and said, "The stock market has crashed." The instructor stood frozen in place for a moment. He finally asked if someone could get some better information. He whispered emphatically, "Get the IBM stock price!" Enron was still fourteen years in the future, so we had everything invested in IBM—our paychecks, our pensions and our stock portfolios. For more than eight decades, IBM's top investor was its own employee-owners.

A Loss of Faith

It was in this environment that John Akers' administrative assistant called. "Pete, I have your Speak Up! in front of me, what's the concern?"

I had spent six months away from my family completing a transition from IBM first-line manager to AS/400 systems engineer. In the branch office, I was surrounded by technical mentors — some of whom had been in IBM for more than thirty-five years. They didn't wait on development to fix problems; they fixed software issues themselves. But IBM had taken its first step down a dangerous path. It offered its top performers two years' salary and $25,000 to take early retirement — a financial incentive that few could or would turn down. IBM's top talent was lining up at the exits. They left to work for our customers, our business partners and even our competitors. Because of this, I had written to the chairman because we seemed to be on the wrong path.

When I went to new manager's school, some of the instructors had a second assignment working Speak Up!s for IBM's CEOs. As they shared their experiences, we were filled with pride in the integrity of our company, sadness for the deep employee troubles we might experience someday, and apprehension at IBM's expectations of its first-line managers. Now John Akers' administrative assistant was on the phone with me, and I was uneasy as I stood at a window of our IBM building overlooking the Austin Hill Country.

"I wasn't sure a Speak Up! was the proper path," I said. "I don't have a complaint; I just wanted to tell someone what is happening in the field because of this retirement offer. Our best folks are preparing to leave the business. Many of us just finished technical training, and we really need these folks to stick around for a while. If they go to the competition, I know I can't compete with them."

He responded, "It's something we need to do, though."

Elephants were finding their way back into our discussions and decisions.

"Why?"

"These are tough economic times."

We talked for quite a while. The details today are blurry except for the final point that is still seared in my memory.

"Why don't we have Opinion Surveys anymore?" I asked. "They meant a lot to us. As a manager, I know it was tough, but it changed me as a person."

He responded, "You know the CEO has tough decisions to make. Those decisions don't always get good reviews, especially from employees who can't understand all the reasons behind them."

"I didn't get good reviews initially either, but I sat down with my team and we worked through it. In the end the feedback made me a better manager, a better person and a better decision maker. It brought us together."

"The feedback we get isn't always positive or helpful," he said.

"You have to work through it," I insisted. "There will always be those who want to complain."

"These are tough decisions we are making right now, and most don't understand," he repeated.

"We understand tough decisions."

"Most can't."

I was beginning to understand why my team hadn't liked my defensiveness as a manager.

I had a sense that this administrative assistant was missing the point, so I asked, "Do you believe that we can't tell the difference between a bad leader making a bad business decision and a good leader making a tough business decision?"

There was silence on the phone. Finally the administrative assistant repeated, "These are tough times."

Until that moment, I had been the one missing the point—upper management no longer had any trust or confidence in us.

My conversation with Akers' assistant was just a sneak preview of what we would eventually discover was a complete lack of faith on the part of the executive leadership in its employees. In April 1991, some executive meeting notes were published in the press, including a memo from John Akers stating that too many employees "were standing around IBM water coolers."

The incident killed company morale. Some blamed the person who leaked it; I blamed our CEO for thinking it. We all knew that if IBM failed, we would not only lose our paychecks, pensions and portfolios, but also our work family. No one was standing around—Mr. Akers had lost sight of how vested every IBMer was in the corporation. We had just heard the equivalent of Jimmy Carter's malaise speech. President Carter was out of touch with the American people and John Akers was out of touch with us.

The Light at the End of the Tunnel

In 1993, Louis V. Gerstner Jr. assumed control. He called us to be the winning team we knew we were. He crushed the idea of splitting up IBM. He established a three-prong revenue strategy—hardware, software and services. But with almost one out of every two full-time IBMers now gone,[5] the stress to keep delivering superlative customer service and support was beyond belief. We leaned on that same IBM family spirit that had delivered across the Great Depression and the twentieth century's other seventeen recessions.

After a final revenue decline of 2.8% in 1993—Mr. Gerstner's first year as CEO—we would deliver six straight years of revenue growth. It was a great turnaround for a great team. Kevin Maney, in *The Maverick and His Machine*, once said that "the core of IBM—its ultimate economic engine—was not information machines; rather, it was its culture,"[6] and unlike John Akers, that's exactly what Gerstner tapped into to support his success—IBM's true economic engine.

We were back.

Endnotes

1   Thomas J. Watson Sr., *Men—Minutes—Money* (IBM Corporation, New York, 1934), p. 218, reprinted with permission of IBM.

2   Thomas J Watson Jr., *Father, Son & Company* (Bantam Books, New York, 1990), p. 303.

3   Marilyn A. Harris, "IBM: More Worlds to Conquer," *BusinessWeek*, February 18, 1985, pp. 84–98.

4   © 2013 Morningstar. All rights reserved. *Morningstar 2013 Ibbotson SBBI Classic Yearbook* (Morningstar Inc., 2013), pp. 158, 184–185, used with permission.

5   From IBM's annual reports of December 31, 1985, and December 31, 1994: IBM's full-time workforce dropped from 405,535 to 219,838.

6   Kevin Maney, *The Maverick and His Machine* (John Wiley and Sons, Inc., New York, 2003), p. 436.

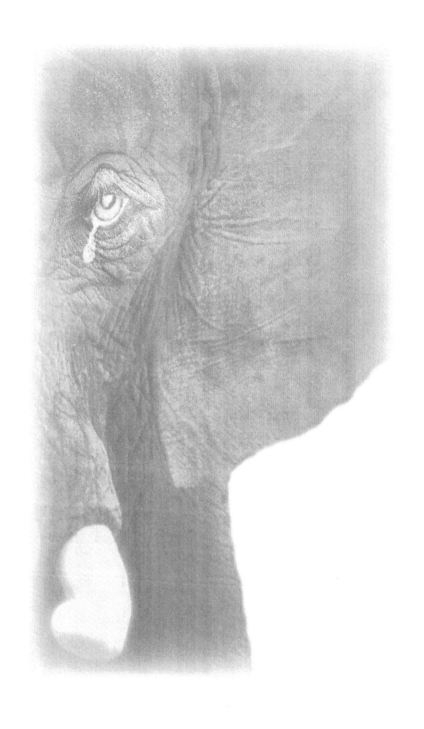

CHAPTER FOUR

THE WATERSHED EVENT

> "When we start thinking of men as automatons, clicking their respective ways through the processes of life with mechanical exactness, that day we lose our own identity and become automatons ourselves. When we cease to realize the interdependence of men we are on the brink of failure."[1]
>
> **Thomas. J. Watson Sr.**, *Men — Minutes — Money*

A Defining Moment

> The [Pension] Fund assets are held in trust for the sole benefit of plan participants and their beneficiaries. IBM is not permitted to use them for corporate operating expenses or for any purpose other than the payment of retirement benefits or plan expenses.[2]
>
> *About Your Benefits*, IBM Personal Pension Plan

> Mr. Gerstner changed the rules of the game on me in the last quarter of my life when I couldn't do anything to change the end result, so I just keep working. It may have been legal, but it wasn't ethical.
>
> **IBMer of nineteen years**

Imagine a high school basketball game between two cross-town rivals. They've been locked in conflict for sixty-two years, and now they're playing yet again for the regional championship.

North High, the visiting team, is fast, short and nimble. They run a full-court defense and look for three-point plays. The home team, Binghamton Central, is tall and methodical. They have a disciplined approach and take high-percentage shots.

Central's coach has recently assumed control of this once-perennial powerhouse that's been falling behind in the last few years. He's rebuilt the team, reenergized individual players and given them the resurgence they so desperately needed.

With two minutes left in the game, and the score tied, both teams return to the court after a time-out. Each looks into their opponent's eyes, hoping to see fatigue or doubt; instead, all they see is courage, strength and determination. Both teams smile. This is their moment. Character has carried them through the season, into the play-offs and to these defining, final few minutes. They both want to win, but they both know, win or lose, that they've proven themselves—a tradition has been preserved.

But Central's new coach is not going to leave his legacy to chance. He strides to the referee, rule book in hand, and points to an archaic regulation left over from the days the three-point shot was first introduced:

"The three-point play may be suspended in the last quarter at the request of either team."

There's confusion on the court as the referees discuss the rule. They know it will hand the championship to Central, but they have no choice—it's in the rules, and perfectly legal. The players listen in disbelief as the ruling is announced. Cries of anger displace the muttered confusion in the hot, overcrowded and emotion-filled stadium.

As expected, Central outdistances North High. But when it's over, there are no cheers, no ovations, no joy. The players just stand silently on the court. The visiting team feels robbed; but the home team is robbed too.

The coach's true loss was in the eyes of his players.

For though the scoreboard flashes a win, it is not their win.

Some would see nothing wrong with this coach's actions; to them, he won the game.

Some would see an ethical catastrophe; to them, something more precious than a game was at risk.

But none would deny the coach's true loss that day, reflected in the eyes of his players.

Lou's Pep Talk

When Lou Gerstner joined Big Blue, he called for volunteers to create a new IBM. I immediately signed up to be a "Gerstner Guerilla." I wanted him to know I was one of those dedicated to bringing IBM back from the edge. I fired up my 3270 green-screen e-mail system and sent him a message saying, "Count me in! I am in this game."

He responded in the December 1993 issue of *THINK* magazine with an open letter thanking the hundreds of us who responded. He wrote that he needed five thousand IBMers who were:

- Committed to the long-term success of all IBM in a fast-changing, intensely competitive global business environment. Commitment to your career and to your business unit [was] not enough.

- Zealous in making things work for the customer, especially when the customer's needs require the involvement of several different parts of IBM. Turf barons and baronesses need not apply.

- Undeterred by bureaucracy, obstacles and this-is-the-way-we've-always-done-things thinking. [He was] looking for people with the guts to go above, below, around or through internal hurdles.

- Willing to take risks in the face of conventional wisdom and practice.

- Constantly looking at everything we [did] with a critical eye, finding new ways to do things better and more productively. [He needed] people who [spent] company money as prudently as they [spent] their own money and resources.

- Looking to the future with confidence. (No handwringers!)[3]

He closed it out saying, "I'd be proud to have you at my side as we move forward."

IBM leadership had returned! We had found a leader who like the Watsons believed "the first step toward leadership was not legislation, but spirit."[4] I had never stopped working, never stopped giving of myself to the company that defined a different way of doing business. And now someone was once again talking to our heart and soul. It was the pep talk before the start of the big game, and we were ready to take the court.

Pounding the Courts

We were not rookies. IBM had survived many a twentieth-century financial crisis: Tom Watson Sr. carried IBM through nine recessions and the Great Depression; Tom Watson Jr. transitioned a family business into a modern corporation through three recessions. And none of those, nor the three recessions endured by Frank Cary or John Opel, were easy to navigate. In describing IBM's near death experience in 1965, Watson Jr. said:

Those were terrible days, because the more we dug into it, the worse the situation looked—which is always what happens in a crisis. Opel [at this time a young executive in the Data Processing Division] finally got so frustrated that he insisted that each factory manager take a physical inventory—which means clerks with clipboards walking through the factories counting things.... We had almost six hundred million dollars of work-in-process inventory.... Understating the inventory made it seem as though IBM had more cash on hand than we actually had. In reality the 360 [the IBM mainframe] had soaked up all our funds. In another few weeks we'd have needed emergency loans to meet the payroll.[5]

Many of these employees were still working for IBM when Gerstner became CEO—it was a time of thirty-, forty- and fifty-year employee service. Even with early retirements, he had an experienced set of first-string players and a deep bench to face any economic crisis.

And by his sixth year, in 1999, we were soaring again: revenue grew 40%, to $87.5 billion; combined net income reached $33 billion (more than the preceding twelve years combined); IBM stock underwent two 2-for-1 splits; and full-time head count rebounded 40%. These were heady times, as IBM's stock, its revenue, its net income, its cash flow and its image all went up.[6]

Together, we made Lou's elephant dance. We praised him in customer meetings for providing us with focus, determination and enthusiasm. We raised him over our shoulders for keeping IBM together, for preserving the IBM brand, for putting the customer first and for building a new hardware, software and services strategy. I and others praised him for all these decisions that he takes ample credit for in his book, as well as one he seems not to acknowledge, even to this day: he tapped into something special—IBM's eight-decade-old culture—which was always there, just dormant for a while.

As Kevin Maney put it, "The culture's adhesive preserved loyalty even if the leader faltered, or the company seemed to make a wrong turn. Employees didn't want to leave this family if something went wrong. Instead, they wanted to stay and work to make it better. The culture bought Watson a margin of error."[7]

The Watson culture bought Mr. Gerstner time, too. It was not in our DNA to head to the exits early. In more than eighty years IBM had never abandoned us, and we wouldn't abandon IBM. Because of our history, we believed Mr. Gerstner's words; we believed he was walking alongside us.

In *Who Says Elephants Can't Dance?* Mr. Gerstner seems offended—as an outsider from RJR Nabisco—that we referred to him as "cookie man." Maybe, because of this, he thought we weren't supporting him. Respect for true leadership resides in the heart though, not nicknames. IBMers called Mr. Watson the "old man" and his son "junior." Yes, we made jokes about cookie man; then again IBMers joked about everything, including Watson Sr.'s 1940s "Songs of The IBM."[8]

But what happened next was not a laughing matter.

Gerstner's New Game Plan

In 1999, after achieving financial stability and with a U.S. pension plan that was overfunded by $7 billion,[9] IBM's senior vice president of human resources sent an e-mail to all U.S. employees advising them that effective July 1 IBM was converting its U.S. defined-benefit pension plan to a cash-balance plan.

The implications of this change were not readily apparent. Pension plans are complex financial instruments, and it takes an actuarial genius to interpret the impact of most changes to them. But it did not take long for a small group of vocal IBMers to understand how much they stood to lose: most understood they would need to work years longer to reach retirement; many realized they would never be able to retire, or would have to retire with a reduced standard of living; some grasped the concept of a "wear away" period (an industry term describing the time it takes just to "break even" after a conversion); most failed to notice that they had lost their retirement health care. But all employee-owners realized that the change impacted them in some way, that they had no choice and that their company had become just another corporation like the rest.

The pension plan changes of the nineties affected 140,000 U.S. employees,[10] almost half (45.5%) of the worldwide, full-time IBM population. With the setting up of a new Yahoo! website to disseminate information, instead of 5,000 Gerstner Guerillas there were now thousands of IBMers using guerilla warfare to fight an internal corporate change—a first in IBM's eighty-five-year history. These employee-owners wrote, called and petitioned their government representatives. Within a few months the brightest of spotlights was placed on cash-balance conversions, a topic barely discussed in the news media before. Congressional hearings were scheduled, detailed reports were requested, and the IRS got involved (placing a moratorium on conversions).

Less than three months after his decision, Gerstner finally buckled under the pressure.[11] But he only buckled halfway. A simple amendment offered a choice between the two plans, but only to individuals forty years of age or older with more than ten years of service. Even with this change, more than half (53.5%) of the U.S. employees still had their future retirement plans forcibly altered—78,000 IBMers live today with drastically altered pensions and no or reduced retirement medical plans.[12] Some were friends of mine who at the time were thirty-nine years old with nineteen years of service.

If Mr. Gerstner had just offered a choice to everyone at the outset, there would have been no furor and probably few complaints—just as there hadn't been in response to all the other pension changes of the previous ten years (see Appendix E)—and the result would have been more retirement dollars flowing into IBM's coffers, with less controversy. Instead, Gerstner made the proverbial mistake of dropping a live frog into boiling water.

In *Who Says Elephants Can't Dance?* there is no discussion of this decision, just a short rationalization implying that if a change only affects a minority of employees, maybe it shouldn't matter:

> Some of these benefit changes created a great furor among a small group of IBM employees.[13]

But it was not a great furor among a small group of IBM employees—rather, it was a great furor among a *very large* group of IBM employees. Although it arrived too late, U.S. Senator Bernie Sanders (Vermont) documented the effects of a cash-balance conversion. He requested a study using the congressional retirement plan as a benchmark. The study documented losses ranging from 30% to 75% if a similar plan had been forced on Congress.[14] Marie Cocco of *Newsday* wrote, "Sanders' own benefit would be cut by 72 percent under a cash-balance formula."[15]

From this congressional report, (See Fig. 3, p. 75) it is easy to visualize the impact of the 1999 pension changes, and to understand why so many employee-owners were so angry at a policy change that was unnecessary for the competitive or financial health of the company.*

It is apparent, though, that IBM's new leadership was determined to hoard the benefits of our renewed growth. Actions contradicted words. IBM divided into "us" and "them." Mr. Gerstner's game plan was to quit sharing the wealth with the company's employee-owners.

Extending the Game Plan

After making this monumental change, Gerstner left IBM in early 2002 and the chief executive role fell to Samuel J. Palmisano. Provided with a new corporate rule book, Palmisano finished what his predecessor had started. In 2006 he sent another e-mail, announcing the elimination of any future defined-benefit accruals for those still working under the old retirement plan. This produced a second pension-funded financial windfall for IBM's top executives:

> In early 2006, IBM announced that it would freeze the pensions of about 117,000 U.S. employees starting in 2008, citing pension costs, volatility, and unpredictability. Only by drilling into its pension filings would one notice that 134 million, or a quarter of its U.S. pension expense the prior year, resulted from pensions for several thousand of its highest-paid people.... The only U.S. pensions dragging down earnings are the executive pensions, which have continued to rise.... In the years since the freeze was announced, **the gains from curtailing benefits have added nearly 3 billion to IBM's income.** [Emphasis added.][16]

---

* For more details on the intricacies of such a conversion — including the personal self-interests that drove these changes in corporate America — I recommend *Retirement Heist: How Companies Plunder and Profit from the Nest Eggs of American Workers* by Ellen E. Schultz (Penguin Group, New York, 2011).

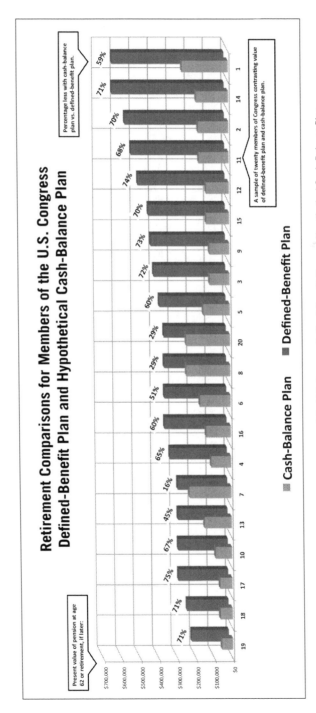

Fig.3 Retirement Comparisons for Members of the U.S. Congress Defined-Benefit Plan and Hypothetical Cash-Balance Plan

IBM ended 2008 with record revenue, record earnings per share, record pre-tax earnings and record free cash flow—all padded with pension plan money.

Unfortunately, in the constant pursuit of ever-better earnings per share, IBM's culture of trust and confidence took a worldwide pounding. After using the United States as its proving ground, IBM's Finance and Human Resources departments reached across the pond. IBMers around the world—mostly oblivious to what was happening in the United States—got a rude awakening.

Profit, as the point of corporate life, was the elephant in the room.

On the tenth anniversary of the U.S. defined-benefit conversion, IBM pulled its retirement benefit out from underneath 28% of its UK workforce.

> With an email sent to employees at about 5:30 pm UK time—after most employees had likely gone home for the day—IBM UK and Ireland general manager Brendon Riley announced the end of the company's Defined Benefit pension scheme, which would have guaranteed retired employees a predefined portion of their final salary.[17]

A true sense of betrayal and outrage emerged as IBM threw its long-term employees into a life-altering event in the last few minutes of their working lifetimes. The employees responded by burning their Quarter Century Club certificates outside IBM laboratories.[18]

Still not satiated, IBM Finance and Human Resources returned to their U.S. test bed in December 2012 to modify the *newest* retirement plan—the IBM 401(k) Plus plan. The internal e-mail from the senior VP of human resources, after stating that IBM's 401(k) plans were "among the best in the industry," said:

> You must be employed on December 15 of each year to receive your IBM contribution for that year. For eligible IBMers, the IBM match and automatic contribution will be deposited to your account on December 31, 2013 (and on the last business day of each subsequent year).

The press seized on this change: "Any employee who leaves IBM's employment prior to December 15 for any reason other than a formal retirement will not receive any company match to his or her own 401(k) contributions for the entire year. Nada!"[19] It was a prophetic observation: they weren't just talking about people leaving the company anymore, but also the now-regular "resource actions," too. At the time I worked for an IBM business partner. When IBM resourced our representative a few months after this announcement, he lost six months of retirement matching dollars. And IBM, in his case, reduced its separation expenses by 15% through another retirement plan change.

The twenty-first-century IBM leadership has for the last fifteen years gradually dismantled one of Watson Sr.'s greatest selfless acts of true service—establishing and funding the IBM Retirement System.

He is turning over in his grave.

Did the Elephant Dance?

Asking an IBMer about Lou Gerstner is like administering a Rorschach test. His inkblot reveals such divergent opinions because vested financial interests are at its epicenter; because some believe words and others actions; because some worry about reputation and others character; and because some live by legalities and others ethics. When the unethical substitute rationalization for intent, some believe the rationalization out of respect for authority; some believe it when they see it in print; some surrender under its constant repetition; and still others believe because it is in their vested interest. But those who suffer its effects can never believe.

Entering the twenty-first century, IBM needed more than financial wizardry: it needed a leader with strength of character and humility. The day Lou was announced, we knew his job would be difficult. We listened to his words. We accepted him. We were willing to do what it took. We supported him, and our families supported us. We worked with our peers into the nights, early mornings and weekends to salvage our company. He had our commitment and support. Bringing IBM back was not his executive battle; it was our family war.

Yet, with the publication of *Who Says Elephants Can't Dance?*, Gerstner documented what we had grown to know: he never tried to understand the Watsons' culture and he never attributed any of his success to their beliefs. In his book when he describes the Basic Beliefs he lists:

- Excellence in everything we do,
- Superior customer service, and
- Respect for the Individual.[20]

In the thirty years I worked at IBM, I never saw Respect listed last.

If Gerstner's elephant ever danced, it does so no longer. IBM's actions of the last fifteen years have inserted the profit elephant into every room. Jim Collins' premise that the world's greatest corporations treat profit like food for the body—necessary but not the point of life—no longer rings true within the twenty-first-century IBM.[21] Instead, IBM's core ideology has become the maximization of shareholder wealth. The company has become gluttonous, and as in the human body, gluttony has deleterious effects on long-term health.

Many believe that IBM is doing great. Many believe IBM is soaring in the twenty-first century. I don't know if IBM will fail financially, but I do know IBM is not living up to its potential, and that when the next test comes—and economic tests are a capitalistic certainty—the Watsons' deep blue cultural currents will not be present to push ever onward.

IBM's Constitution had proven itself over eight decades, six CEOs, eight stock market declines, sixteen recessions and the Great Depression. In contrast, more than eight years of economic expansion powered by the greatest bull market run in history supported Gerstner's first one hundred months. With the U.S. economy filling his sails and the employee-owner driving his corporation forward, Mr. Gerstner replaced our Corporate Constitution with a vacuum.

His actions surpassed even the Watsons' margin of error. He brought us to the edge of an unprecedented precipice—IBM's first cultural crisis.

Endnotes

1 Thomas J. Watson Sr., *Men—Minutes—Money* (IBM Corporation, New York, 1934), p. 90, reprinted with permission of IBM.

2 *About Your Benefits*—IBM Personal Pension Plan—Prior Plan January 1, 2005, document number: USHR113.

3 Louis V. Gerstner, "Think Twice, Open Letter to IBM Employees," *THINK*, December 1993.

4 Thomas Graham Belden and Marva Robins Belden, *The Lengthening Shadow* (Little, Brown, Boston, 1962), p. 196.

5 Thomas J. Watson Jr., *Father, Son & Company* (Bantam Books, New York, 1990), p. 358.

6 Mergent Industrial Manual, International Business Machines Corporation, 1989 through 2000.

7 Kevin Maney, *The Maverick and His Machine* (John Wiley and Sons, Inc., New York, 2003), p. 342.

8 Personal interview with ninety-five-year-old IBMer.

9 Ellen E. Schultz, *Retirement Heist: How Companies Plunder and Profit from the Nest Eggs of American Workers* (Penguin Group, New York, 2011), p. 9.

10 Mary Williams Walsh, "What If a Pension Shift Hit Lawmakers Too," *New York Times*, March 9, 2003.

11 "Big Blue Doubles Number of Employees Eligible for Old Benefits Plan," *CNNMoney*, September 17, 1999.

12 "IBM Does an About-Face on Pensions," *New York Times*, September 18, 1999.

13 Louis V. Gerstner Jr., *Who Says Elephants Can't Dance?* (Harper Business, New York, 2002), p. 102.

14 Patrick Purcell, *Estimated Benefit Under a Cash Balance Plan* (Congressional Research Report, February 11, 2003) pp. 1–4.

15 Marie Cocco, *The High Cost of a Corporate Low-Ball Tactic, Newsday*, April 2003.

16 Ellen E. Schultz, *Retirement Heist: How Companies Plunder and Profit from the Nest Eggs of American Workers* (Penguin Group, New York, 2011), p. 103.

17 Cade Metz, "IBM UK Snuffs 'Final Salary' Pensions," *Register*, July 7, 2009.

18 "IBM Pension Report," *BBC South Today*, BBC News, July 2009.

19 Helaine Olen, "IBM Makes Changes to Its 401(k) Plan," *Forbes*, December 10, 2012.

20 Louis V. Gerstner Jr., *Who Says Elephants Can't Dance?* (Harper Business, New York, 2002), p. 184.

21 James C. Collins and Jerry I. Porras, *Built to Last: Successful Habits of Visionary Companies* (Harper Business, New York, 1994), p. 55.

CHAPTER FIVE

A FLOUNDERING SHIP

> " We have devoted a lot of thought to giving men employment. We are employing more people today than we employed in 1929 and I am mighty thankful that this is so. We have let out some people, but we have put more on. And I am sure that you men have not let out anybody that was deserving of his job. As long as you run on that basis, whether it is good times or bad times, you are running on the right basis. When your men get it in their hearts that they have something they could not go around the corner and get, that they have a company back of them that has some heart and wants to help them, your troubles are over."[1]
>
> **Thomas J. Watson Sr.**

The New IBM Family Days

In *Who Says Elephants Can't Dance?* Gerstner wrote, "If we have too many people, let's right-size fast; let's get it done by the end of the third quarter."[2] He was talking about 1993, his first year as IBM's CEO.

The press had said of this layoff strategy:

> New IBM Chairman Louis V. Gerstner Jr. announces an $8.9 billion charge against 2nd quarter 1993 earnings to fund a massive cost-cutting program, under which IBM will lay off 35,000 employees, send 25,000 more into early retirement.... Gerstner tells reporters over lunch that he intends the bold move to end IBM's recent practice of cutting its payroll incrementally quarter after quarter, a practice Gerstner calls "Chinese water torture."[3]

Two decades later, in 2013, Senior VP and CFO Mark Loughridge discussed a different layoff philosophy with analysts — now referring to them as workforce balancing actions:

> However, given our first quarter performance, we now expect to take the bulk of our workforce balancing actions for the year in the second quarter, as opposed to last year when it was distributed across the quarters.[4]

"Right-sizing" was the 1990s' politically correct term for layoffs. Unfortunately the size never proved quite right. IBM layoffs, which are usually executed over a period of twenty-four hours, have been quarterly, continual, persistent and arbitrary for more than twenty years. Internally IBMers refer to them as Resource Action Days or, more poetically, R.A. Days. Such days are never about him, her or me; they are always about us. They are the twenty-first century's new IBM Family Day.

My family experienced two such days in 2003, within a few months of each other.

Out of the Blue

In January my new sales manager called me at my home office. "Pete, layoffs may be hitting the Sales and Distribution Division (S&D). You've been a wonderful employee, you've performed well, and I'm giving you as much time as I can, but you are on my list to be targeted for a layoff. If you haven't found another job in the next thirty days, you will get the Letter."

"The Letter" rang in my ears.

I had never seen the Letter. But at the time, it was the Mark of Cain — by next month you would be gone.

My stomach tightened. I heard a question escape: "Why me?"

"You're just at the wrong place at the wrong time. They've decided they don't want traveling sales reps anymore. They're eliminating the remote coverage out of Austin, and as you know, we already have someone in Austin covering central Texas."

I thought back to my decision to cover the Midwest United States. I had relinquished Central Texas to an Austin newlywed. I had always traveled anyway. My wife and I had gotten used to it, and since many of my peers would not travel, it meant job security. Now I was in trouble because of it.

"Will you support me looking for another job?" I asked.

"Pete, sure I will, but since you didn't make quota last year, you're now rated a 3. That limits your options. You can only move within the Sales and Distribution Division. No other IBM division will take a poor performer."

I could feel the noose tightening — "poor performer" set off alarms. As always, a 1 walks on water, a 4 needs to look for work. What I was about to learn was that a 3 also put up impregnable barriers.

"But my last 3 was almost eighteen years ago. I was just giving direct sales a try."

"The only appraisal that counts is the one this year."

This was a new breed of IBM manager, with a new set of supporting rules. His hands were tied. He had no leverage, no authority to make exceptions. He was powerless.

"I thought I was in the Software Group?" I stammered. "All my executive contacts are there. In Software Group, I could call in favors."

It was hard to tell if this conversation affected him or not — he responded very factually, "Pete, you're in Sales and Distribution. With this appraisal you'll need the approval of the accepting division's senior vice president to move. I'm sorry, Pete."

"Senior vice president" meant one of the CEO's direct reports. The more I twisted and turned, the tighter the noose drew.

But he was giving me a head start. I held my breath as I asked, "If another manager calls you, I'll need you to tell them that my 3 rating is just because I didn't make quota in some pretty tough years; that my performance, other than making quota, is exemplary. Are you comfortable with that statement?"

"No problem, Pete. Your appraisal is about missing quota. Nothing personal, it's just the condition of IBM sales right now. Not many folks are getting good appraisals."

Now I had to face the next hurdle. Somehow the division I worked in had changed. For the previous two years, I had been isolated in my home office. I worked alone with no face-to-face contact with my manager or any executives. The home office had become my greatest liability. I might as well have been in a different company.

The first week passed in a blur as I fumbled around IBM's archaic internal job application system — a 1980s mainframe remnant. S&D was buttoned up tight. Even offers to relocate at my own expense fell on deaf ears. It became obvious that jobs were filled before being posted — experienced managers ensuring they had their candidate in the queue. I lost precious time working within a broken system.

Through all of this my wife stood by my side. She constantly said, "We will get through this." My kids never knew what was going on, but they heard my temper flare and my patience grow shorter.

I needed to find people who knew my history. I had to put my relationships to work. For several days I worked the IBM organization chart. I started at the CEO level and worked my way through every executive I had worked with and could possibly call up for assistance. I needed one of them to take my case forward. Then I called peers in their organizations that I knew. I needed to find an unpublished job opening.

Jobs were disappearing everywhere. S&D was hit the hardest. I called for days, working my way through all my old contacts. Many said they had been getting similar calls. Many said, emotionally, that they had nothing and knew of nothing. Most treated it with disbelief.

Some said, "Pete, IBM won't let that happen to you."

They thought in twentieth-century terms, as if IBM were still a living, breathing, caring being.

I would say, "If I don't have a job by the time they print that package, I'm history." But as I felt the pain I was causing, I would add, "I'll make it. Keep me in mind if you hear of anything opening up. I'll check back." I turned fifty that year—a scary time to be starting over again. But I kept at it.

Suddenly, I found one! After hundreds of calls, a single chance at continued employment. Donna Briar and I had worked together when I was the OS/2 Warp Server brand manager and again on the OS/2 worldwide sales and support teams. There was a market management position open on her team. I asked if she would recommend me.

"Pete, my God, are you kidding?"

"Has it been posted yet?"

"I don't think so. The person is just leaving."

This was the first positive sign in almost two weeks. I had found that elusive unadvertised opening and I was the first in line.

John Carter was a vice president in Software Group (SWG). I had never worked directly for him, but I had been constantly around him in meetings, consultations and critical decisions during my tenure as Warp Server brand manager. We worked together again as we extended OS/2's life with Workspace on Demand. With many self-doubts, I called him directly.

"John, I don't know if you would remember me or not, this is Pete Greulich."

"Pete, it's great to hear from you." The instant recognition caught me by surprise. "Donna told me you would be calling. What can I do?"

All I could think was how much I owed Donna right then.

"John, I'm looking for work." I didn't want to get into the desperation I was feeling.

"I have an opening," he said. "You need to get with my first-line manager, though. I'll give him a call, but you know it's his team and I won't tell him to hire you. You'll have to pass his interview."

"I understand, John. That's all I can ask."

The clock kept ticking. I didn't know the first-line manager, and my interview with him was at IBM's annual software training in Las Vegas. It turned out I was one of hundreds looking for work at the event. It had morphed from an education event into an internal job fair. The desperation was rampant. It consumed one-on-one conversations; it echoed down every hallway; you heard it in every hushed "You too?" It was a bloodbath, even as executives stood in our midst and declared on stage how great a year we had in front of us.*

When I met John's first-line manager for my interview, it started off ablaze: "You know John told me I don't have to hire you. He was real clear about that."

Was he judging my reaction? Was this the "stress question" that we had all been taught in new manager's school? If so, it was working. Fear crept in. This was my only opportunity. I couldn't go home empty-handed.

I responded quickly, "I expected as much. I don't like folks that use executive pressure to get jobs. Never cared for the 'good old boy network,' but in this case I happened to know both Donna and John. I hope you don't feel like you got caught in the middle. I absolutely know it is still your decision."

He immediately lightened up. "Well, according to John you are the closest person to someone who walks on water in this company, so let's talk."

Two days before the letter was slated to arrive, Software Group approved my return.

Musical Chairs

Unfortunately, I had only experienced the first downbeat in a Texas two-step. The second came sixty days later, when rumors began circulating that another round of layoffs was imminent. Then a date was leaked.

I went into John's office. "John, it's hard to take another layoff threat so soon. Are we on tap for tomorrow? If so, I need to prepare my family for

---

* As a dancing elephant gains experience, it perfects its step—never again would there be a chance to look for work in this manner. The following year the resourced individuals would be unable to attend this event as travel budgets for them would be denied.

another round. You know it'll hit the papers and media. I need to let my wife know. If she heard this at work, after what we just went through—"

"Pete, we are okay," he interrupted. John understood the worry in my voice. "You can't tell anyone, but it isn't our team this time."

The next morning, as my wife was walking out the door, I stopped her and told her she might hear of layoffs in Software Group with a big emphasis on my Tivoli division. I told her it would be a big one—it might even make national news—but that we were okay.

She gazed at me hard as if to discern any hidden fear.

I repeated firmly, "We are not affected."

Not sensing anything, she said, "Thank you, if I had seen this on the news, I'm not sure what my reaction would have been. It would be hard to stay focused on teaching. I would be worried about you."

"It's still going to be a hard day," I said.

The layoffs made the morning news. It went national quickly. People's lives became statistics. I couldn't face my coworkers. I had seen too many cry in bathrooms, stand shell-shocked outside of a first-line manager's door or leave work early to tell their families.

So I left early—nothing productive ever gets done on R.A. Days anyway.

That afternoon, I looked up from my home office desk to see my wife standing at the door. Her face was as white as a ghost. I thought someone had died.

"What's wrong?" I asked.

"You're supposed to be at work. You told me this morning...." Her voice dropped to an almost inaudible level, but I could see the question formed by her lips, "Is it starting again?"

"My God, no! I just came home early. It was just too hard to watch everyone being told. It didn't affect us."

There was no glee in my voice. It would have been disrespectful to those who were at home having a different conversation with

R.A. Days were a family affair.

their spouses. Seeing her physical discomfort I added, "Not financially anyway."

She came into my office and sat stiffly on the edge of the couch.

"When I saw you were home, when I saw your car in the garage," her voice faltered, "I got sick in the downstairs bathroom."

I touched her hand and said, "I'm so sorry. You were so strong before. I never knew you were affected so deeply by what we went through."

She paused for a moment. "Until this moment, neither did I." No tears flowed, but they swelled up in her eyes as she recalled the details of just two months prior.

The homeless elephant in the room — twenty-one years after Tom and my coworkers removed it — had returned. My wife felt it. I did, too. But until then we had never acknowledged it.

The New Corporate Carpe Diem

The resource actions never ended. Gerstner started them; Samuel J. Palmisano became addicted to them; Virginia M. Rometty, evidently, sees them as the only path to meeting the 2015 EPS road map. For the individual, resource actions are water torture, and for a corporate social ecology they are waterboarding. When in process, they are suffocating. They touch moms and dads, aunts and uncles, brothers and sisters. These elephants are a family affair, and they touch us everywhere — sometimes it is distant; sometimes it is close; sometimes it is on your doorstep.

On January 21, 2009, I decided to capture one on paper.

The day began in the Jewish tradition — in the darkness of the night before. Our CEO sent an e-mail prologue, most likely as he left for home, family and friends.

> Dear IBMer:
> We have just issued our financial results for the fourth quarter and full year 2008.... Our 2008 results set several records: record revenue of $103.6 billion—the first time IBM has passed the $100 billion mark; record pre-tax earnings of $16.7 billion, up 15 percent from 2007; record earnings per share of $8.93; and record free cash flow of $14.3 billion.[5]
> **Sam Palmisano**, Chairman, President and Chief Executive Officer

With the rising sun, his words again celebrated the previous year's financial results on our intranet home page: "We transformed the IBM Company and you can see it in our financial performance.... If we hadn't there is no way '08 would have been record, record, record."[6]

But few of us cared, because within the next twelve hours a large number of us—the whisper number was seventeen thousand—would receive career-ending pink slips. So we feared a different kind of record—being one among the largest number of employees resourced in a single day in IBM's most profitable division.

My closest friends were reaching out by breakfast.

David was first. Where he lived it was 7:30 a.m. He was on the technical team that supported me. It was a short instant message: "I got hit by the latest resource action." I asked for his résumé. When I called a manager—a personal friend—he apologized: "Human Resources told me that if I fill my open position with a person from the resource action I'll have to 'ante up' a replacement from my own team. Pete, I can't do that." (That afternoon, an IBM spokesperson told the Austin press, "Some employees could find other positions within IBM and we're enabling them in that effort."[7] Apparently a spokesperson's "some could" should be translated to "none will.")

Helen was next. We were teammates. She and I had traveled the world together. Every country we entered, she looked for presents for my wife—pashminas in China, pewter in Malaysia and Bidriware in India. Her father had died recently, and she moved her mom near her. We always compared notes and laughed over the day-to-day problems of the sandwich generation—caring for young children and aging parents at the same time. She was, like so many women today, balancing the duties of wife, mother and daughter-caretaker. Sadness set in as I felt that I was losing the best of friends and remembered a bygone era that had seen me through such life events.

Roger was on our team, too. I had recommended he join it. I now regretted that advice. I learned that HR's lightning could scorch the same place twice.

Terry was a friend of twenty years. He was told to retire, though he still had a son to put through college. In January 1993 he had found a job for me—a move to brand management. It breathed new life into my IBM career. He sought me out then, but I couldn't help him now. I felt powerless, embarrassed and full of guilt.

The Linux worldwide sales team was disbanded. Many of my closest and oldest friends were there. If there was any group of IBMers that had epitomized a nineties Gerstner Guerilla team, it was us—we found seven more years of revenue for IBM's largest and best OS/2 banking customers. IBM's Linux strategy lost some amazing expertise. Strategies stumble in the face of an earnings-per-share road map.

By mid-morning the more distant and more desperate called, and the internal grapevine pulsated with information. June coordinated sales and technical education. She made my job easier. She said that her whole team took horrible cuts. She was a sharp, conscientious and hard worker. This day reinforced cynicism—it was not about performance but wrong place, wrong time. The general business team was disbanded. They sold to small and medium businesses through IBM business partners. Nine months later, after a few beers, I would hear one person's estimate that three-quarters of the organization was resourced—everybody but management. I would be told, "It has not been going well since." America's Techline team—the software salesmen's first line of support—was cut in half. Their mission changed because they were shorthanded. This sales process change meant fewer customer proposals, fewer presentations or escalations and more work for the individual sales representative. John was in product testing. Even though our software revenue grew by double digits, our testing department was decimated. Less regression testing meant customers would discover more problems while in production. Katie and Samuel were product managers. An acquisition had brought them into IBM, and an R.A. Day jettisoned them. Two conflicting strategies fought each other, as expertise purchased at a premium was set adrift.

By lunch the statistics started to flow: the Raleigh press reported fourteen hundred jobs lost; the Austin press reported a thousand to fifteen hundred; and both promised more details with the evening news. I thought not. The news would remain off tonight.

After lunch, R.A. Day reached out for me. The previous year, I had been a 1 performer, but in the last few weeks my appraisal had been dropped without explanation. Because of past experience, I believed I was receiving a personal message: "You're on the resource action list."

As I left my desk, I wondered if every now-unanswered instant message had a person behind it who thought I didn't care. Outside it was a warm, sunny day. I picked a spot under some oak trees in a small, quiet park. No matter what happened, I wanted to remember what was important. It wasn't the end of the world; it just wasn't the ending I had planned. It meant that at fifty-five I would be starting down a new path. By now the cuts were so deep that the day's futility and despair had sunk in across the organization. I knew I couldn't even save myself.

Brad, my manager, wasn't on time. Our call was scheduled for 1:15, so I sent him an instant message. He dropped offline.

I wondered if it was him or my BlackBerry. If I was in his shoes right now, how could I call friends and give them the bad news?

At 1:30 my phone rang. When I answered, Brad immediately said, "This is a good call—you're okay. I did my best to set up individual calls with everyone."

Relieved, I asked Brad how he was holding up. Brad was a good man, and I could not imagine carrying his burden. I wanted to tell him it was okay. We all knew it wasn't him doing this to us.

"I've been resourced," he said.

If there is hell on earth, I experienced it that day. I would eventually crawl into bed thanking God the day was done.

As it began in the Jewish tradition, so it ended in the Celtic one, with a wake that everyone handled differently. The emotions ranged as wide as the number of people resourced: from cynicism to stoic acceptance, from fear to frustration, and from disappointment to even cheerfulness at starting a new life. This time, for me, it was anger at the two e-mails—callous epilogues—that arrived at dusk.

The general manager of Tivoli Software wrote:

> Perhaps the best part of a new year is the fresh start we get to refocus on our strategy and goals.... SWG revenues were up 11 percent in 2008 and up 3 percent in the fourth quarter (both at actual rates). Unfortunately, the Tivoli team struggled to reach our double-digit revenue growth goals throughout 2008.... I am proud to say that **the team did a great job of reducing expenses—a continuing high priority for 2009.** [Emphasis added.][8]

The senior VP and group executive of IBM Software Group followed this closely with his expression of gratitude:

> You hit our profit plan for the year, an outstanding achievement that contributed significantly to IBM's growth model. Despite a challenging economic environment, strong sales execution in 4Q helped achieve our best quarter of the year. And we gained market share, although we missed our full-year revenue plan.... **In the quarter, we also did an excellent job controlling expenses. This will continue to be important in 2009** as we shift our investments to advance our growth strategy, deliver results to shareholders and emerge from this unprecedented environment even stronger. [Emphasis added.][9]

In the journal where I captured this day, I wrote, "We know they don't care, but do they not think?"

In 1926, speaking at a Quarter Century Club meeting, Tom Watson Sr. had said:

> Experience is a great teacher and in a highly technical business such as ours it is essential. The longer a man stays with a company the more valuable he should become, and I want to say to the twenty-five-year men that I consider the members of the Quarter Century Club one of the greatest assets our company possesses, because you know what should and should not be done.[10]

I am an IBM Quarter Century Club member. As one of my company's greatest assets and because I know what should and should not be done, what was done that day should *never* be done. It was ruthlessness in a time of corporate plenty.

Although the day's pain passed, the mourning continued over the next month as silence replaced camaraderie with each friend's departure. It continued over the next year, at worldwide sales events, as friends toasted friends "not present." But worst of all, it arrived in the form of hundreds of automated e-mail replies that "this user is not listed in the Domino Directory" until I found the courage to delete their names from my distribution lists.

A Loss of Honor

It was in 1921 that Tom Watson Sr. first set aside a day exclusively to celebrate an employee-owner's twenty-five years of service. If you made it into the exclusive Quarter Century Club, you had proven yourself in one of the world's most rigorous corporate environments. In 1986 I was honored to host such an event in one man's life. It was a day when we, his IBM family, told his personal family what he meant to us. It was a day set aside to describe the times spent with us and away from them. The pride we inspired in his family created a moment to be cherished. As a first-line manager, I would never have a more wonderful experience.

In 2005, my manager asked me how I wanted to celebrate my entrance into this club. It took me a week to respond with this e-mail:

> I have lost a lot of friends to layoffs. Many of those folks were better men than I. The only reason I am still around is because I wasn't at the wrong place at the wrong time, or in the one case when I was I had access to a Vice President to save me. To celebrate an occasion like this, that so many of my friends won't have a chance to experience would be very difficult for me. The day I hit 25 years, I will remember all the folks that called me for help, for a pointer to that person that might have a job opening and I did not have the means to help. Although I know I have always done my best, it never felt like enough. I think I will let the occasion pass quietly. It will be a hard day for me, because there are many I wish were here to celebrate and although I am sure they would not want me to take this approach, it is best.

That manager was Brad. By not celebrating my own landmark event I deprived him of an honor I had once enjoyed, and selfishly, at the beginning of this day, I wondered if I would see thirty years; this R.A. Day held me accountable for that thought. This day was never really about me.

IBM's New Product Life Cycle

A software product has a life cycle. Metaphorically it is conceived, born, raised, and it dies. It leaves its genetic code imbedded in its offspring. As it goes through this life cycle, it is the bond between a corporation and its customer. To the corporate team it is a living, breathing entity: architects birth it, software developers diaper it, support cleans up any mess, and product and market management ensures it grows straight and strong in the right surroundings. To the customer it is an investment of time to evaluate, money to acquire and skills to implement. Careers depend on its success. It is a wonderful experience to sit in a room full of customers when a product is providing true value; when it's being updated with new, relevant functionality; when it's helping a company gain market share.

Otherwise it is a living hell.

By early 2001, IBM had developed from Tivoli's portfolio one of the industry's most scalable software distribution products, called Tivoli Configuration Manager (TCM). Its target audience was Fortune 2000 customers, and it was successful: twenty-six of IBM's largest customers used TCM to manage more than a hundred thousand endpoints each, and it permeated IBM's installed accounts—more than sixteen hundred customers. The product's annual maintenance stream was one of the top revenue contributors to Tivoli's bottom line. For this one product some of our largest customers were paying hundreds of thousands of dollars each month in support and maintenance.

But it was falling behind the competition. The sales force was asking for new functionality and a lighter, more usable product because the hardware and management costs were too high. We started seeing losses to Microsoft, whose product was scaling. In the fastest growth market—mid-sized businesses—we were noncompetitive because we lacked a streamlined installation, ease of use and fast ROI.

The market and product management teams constructed under the code name "Project Leonardo" a major initiative to move TCM ahead of its competition. The meeting to discuss the project was short. The development director said, "TCM is a cash cow. Why should I spend money on a product that is nothing but pure profit?" He believed that products in this market were commodities with low margins, and should be left to others to waste their profits on. We never convinced him otherwise.

From that day, all investment of any significance ceased. We patched the product, shipped fixes, took support calls and fielded customer complaints, but we never again shipped a major release. Against all advice, this executive put the product on life support to await its death.

By early 2003, IBM realized they needed to do something—TCM may have been a commodity, but it was a critical piece in a customer's complex management puzzle. Without TCM, customers purchased the rest of the software stack from our competitors. We lost account control.

To bypass significant investment in TCM, IBM paid $46 million for a privately held Canadian company called Think Dynamics.[11] This, at the time, was less than one-third of TCM's annual maintenance revenue.

Two new products emerged from that acquisition: Tivoli Provisioning Manager (TPM) and Tivoli Intelligent Orchestrator (TIO). They were showcased at the 2003 U.S. Open Tennis Championships. Press and consultants saw the U.S. Open's Data Center dynamically allocate server resources based on Internet demand. When servers weren't providing the latest statistics for a high-visibility match, the processing power searched for a cure for cancer. It was dynamic server provisioning for the cloud, though the term "cloud" did not yet exist.

Unfortunately, this experiment did not produce a cure for cancer, nor did it produce a replacement for TCM. We would ship release after release of TPM and never hit the mark.

In late 2004, we prepared a chart for the Investment Review Board (IRB), a gathering of top IBM executives. The IRB typically attempts to insert a business direction into a group's technical plans in alignment with the company's corporate strategy. In this case, the talking points on the chart were simple enough:

- Every customer needs software distribution and configuration management.
- TCM's revenue is declining precipitously due to lack of investment.
- TPM is not making up the gap.
- We need investment to stop TCM's decline and improve TPM's success rate.

But there would be no proactive action. We would continue to ship more releases that missed the mark because they were made on the cheap. TCM maintenance revenue plummeted as customers left in droves. But still this wasn't enough to get our top executives' attention—Tivoli's growth through acquisition painted a shiny veneer of high performance over almost all other measurements.

In December 2006, we needed strong customer references for an impending Gartner Magic Quadrant evaluation—a head-to-head comparison of software vendors in various market spaces. Gartner's analyses are respected by our customers and used in their evaluations. TPM for Software (TPMfSW) version 5.1 had just shipped, and it was directly positioned to replace TCM.

Tivoli's general manager called a meeting, which he kicked off by stating that layoffs were on the horizon if we didn't turn this product around. All our competitors were expanding—one grew by almost 100% in the last year. We were losing market share (which is to say we were losing customers).

Development stated their facts: TPM was in a disaster situation. Of its more than 150 customers, three-quarters were inactive and the rest were either uninstalled or just entering the planning phase. After almost four years there were only two in production, and only one of these *might* be a reference we could use with Gartner. The development executives could not assure the team that any customer would get into production.

Sales stated their facts. They filled the pipeline with opportunities but lost at every step of the sales cycle: most sales were lost after an initial checklist evaluation, others when the product could not be installed, and the remainder—even after the geography sales team installed the product for the customer—were lost because of usability and stability issues. These teams had communicated these problems to their worldwide leadership for years. The

> **Sales' role in the Twentieth Century IBM**
>
> Tom Watson Sr. when speaking to the Sales Executives Club of New York gave a clear insight into the role of sales in his IBM. He told his audience, "It goes without saying that there is no excuse, no legitimate reason, for any sales manager trying to build a sales organization to sell something that is not of real value to the people who buy it."

worldwide VP of Tivoli Sales was so tired of hearing it that he told his team, "I don't want to see another chart about product deficiencies. We are in the revenue business, not the technology critique business."

So the geography leadership, at the behest of their worldwide executive, added small quantities of the product into each Enterprise License Agreement.* New terminology came into existence—"ELA stuffing" and "shelfware." The only customers buying such products were acquiring them sight unseen. Because of the nature of these contracts, software revenue flowed to TCM's replacement product that had a fundamental flaw: it couldn't replace a product that had been built a decade earlier and been on life support for half that time.

Before the meeting closed, three basic goals were set:

- Achieve ten customer references for the Gartner evaluation.
- Stop developing and focus on "no excuse" deployments.
- Move one TCM customer to TPM.

All goals were missed. In its 2007 *Magic Quadrant for PC Life Cycle Configuration Management*, Gartner dropped IBM from consideration

---

* An enterprise license agreement (ELA) is a long-term software contract between IBM and one of its customers. ELAs were originally created for mainframe software only, but they have expanded to include other software.

with this short line: "IBM did not meet the reference requirements for this Magic Quadrant because we have not found any organizations using TPMfSW for managing PCs."[12]

TCM and its successor product were now officially dead.

And now, because IBM disregarded customer feedback from its own sales force, had a financial system that found a way to fund failing products, and lacked turnaround development leadership, there was only one option left: break out the checkbook.

In July 2010 IBM Tivoli paid approximately $400 million for a privately held software distribution and personal computer endpoint management company.[13] The general manager said that they were making the acquisition because it filled "a critical need for many of our clients." The elephant in the room was that they were trying to fix a problem that had been festering for almost a decade, and they acquired the company that—for the last two years—had become the most proficient at locating and displacing our existing product with ease. That company was BigFix—a company that, interestingly, had also failed to meet Gartner's requirements less than three years earlier. The difference was, they were listening and acting on our customers' needs when we weren't.

So now IBM had made two acquisitions over seven years totaling almost a half-billion dollars, all related to a single product in a single market. Sales died not because of poor salesmen, but because of a leadership team that substituted centralized, authoritarian business decisions for their salesmen's insights. To recover, IBM would spend more on one product (considering the ten-year costs of two acquisitions, mandated support and integration, and the ongoing loss of business) than it had to acquire the entire Tivoli portfolio.*

IBM's twenty-first-century investments are not the kind that will take IBM into the twenty-second century. IBM's leadership promises billion-dollar investments ad nauseam: Watson,[14] Linux,[15] Global Cloud Footprint,[16] flash storage,[17] new mainframe technology,[18] PureSystems,[19] social collaboration,[20] SMB financing[21] along with job cuts.[22] These are

---

* Tivoli went public in 1995, and a year later IBM acquired the company for $743 million.

not Jim Collins' Big Hairy Audacious Goals[23] set in alignment with business values, but merely press platitudes. Meanwhile the company loses billions in revenue and ignores its internal businesses before setting them adrift.

IBM needs to develop the leadership and internal fortitude to turn around its businesses; otherwise, when the time comes that it must once again reinvent itself, the needed skills will not exist. Its leadership is no longer of the type that made the transition from coffee grinders to tabulating machines to mainframes; that company's leadership spent $5.25 billion on the System/360 in 1966 — ten times net income. An equivalent investment today would be $170 billion.

When Watson Sr. took over C-T-R, his reputation was suspect but his character solid. One of his corporation's twentieth-century remnants — its reputation — is still intact, but its top leadership's character is now suspect.

And because history is repeating itself, IBM will need its strongest leadership in almost a half century if it is to survive.

A Blue Déjà Vu

Virginia M. Rometty, today's chairman, president and CEO, told her sales force after a disappointing first quarter in 2013, "You must respond to customers within twenty-four hours." She might as well have said, "Stop standing around the IBM water coolers."

As IBM financially soars into the twenty-first century, how could this inspire déjà vu of the late eighties? Does IBM have yet another chief executive who can't see facts through her employee-owners' eyes? Could our CEO and our board of directors be mistaken again?

Let's take another look at the mistakes of Opel and Akers, as discussed in Chapter 3.

Has the Current Leadership Set an Unachievable Market Expectation?

IBM is no longer a sales organization. IBM's twenty-first-century CEOs are no longer salesmen-in-chiefs.† They run a financial organization

---

† Watson Sr., later in his life, was often referred to as the World's Greatest Salesman. He was always IBM's salesman-in-chief.

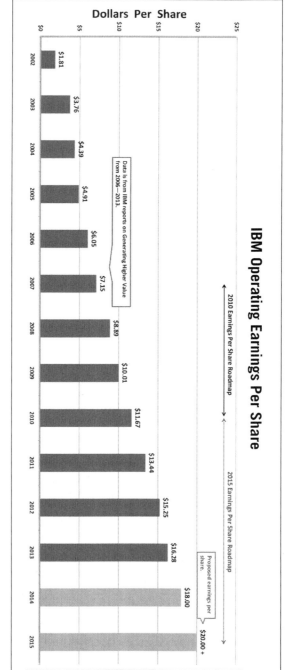

IBM Operating Earnings Per Share

Dollars Per Share

Data is from IBM reports on Generating Higher Value from 2006—2013.

2010 Earnings Per Share Roadmap

2015 Earnings Per Share Roadmap

Proposed earnings per share.

Year	Earnings
2002	$1.81
2003	$3.76
2004	$4.39
2005	$4.91
2006	$6.05
2007	$7.15
2008	$8.89
2009	$10.01
2010	$11.67
2011	$13.44
2012	$15.25
2013	$16.28
2014	$18.00
2015	$20.00 +

Fig. 4 IBM Operating Earnings Per Share

focused on profit expressed as earnings per share (EPS). (See Fig.4, p.100) On this path, you don't have to deliver the right products with the right features at the right time through the right channels. Instead, at least for the short run, fiscal knobs can be tweaked, twisted and tuned to achieve the goal.

But an earnings-per-share discussion is a single-threaded, short-term conversation with one investor — the stockholder. It leaves all other investors out of the dialogue. This can endanger a corporation's long-term success. With the current financial market's emphasis on shareholder value, it bears repeating that Tom Watson Jr. understood this when he wrote that we, as an IBM family, had an obligation to provide an *attractive* return on invested capital.[24] It takes strong executive leadership to balance obligations between all stakeholders: customers, stockholders, employees and the society in which they cohabit.

IBM met the 2010 Road Map a year early. Through financial management, they will meet the 2015 Road Map, too. But meeting these stockholder objectives will risk IBM's credibility with its other stakeholders.

Is the Current Leadership Depleting a Valuable Resource?

As do most corporations, IBM conducts internal employee surveys. They benchmark these results against IT industry averages and the industry's best. In IBM's *2010 Corporate Responsibility Summary,*[25] after citing the company's history of understanding employees' issues and concerns and acting on such concerns, IBM published the following statistics:

Global Pulse Survey Year	2006	2007	2008	2009	2010
Employee Satisfaction (%)	67	69	67	69	65

The report notes — without stating the exact numbers — that the industry benchmarks also declined in 2010. What is not noted in the IBM Corporate Responsibility Survey — and should have been to warrant its title — is that through Q3 2010, IBM North America was significantly below the industry averages in **every category measured**.

In the North American IT industry, nine out of ten employees working in the best organizations said they would recommend their company as a great place to work. The industry average was seven out of ten. In some IBM divisions, barely one in two said they would recommend IBM, and the results were trending in the wrong direction.

It gets even worse when you look at these numbers within a historical context. In the 1986 IBM Opinion Survey an equivalent question was asked:

"How would you rate IBM as a company to work for compared with other companies you know about?"

1986 Opinion Survey	Number of Respondents	—Percentage of Respondents— Favorable	Neutral	Unfavorable
IBM Workgroup (my team)	12	100	0	0
Administrative Branch Office	50	98	2	0
Sales Branch Office	144	98	2	0
IBM Area Administration	715	97	3	0
IBM SW Administration	3686	95	4	0

Not nine out of ten, but ninety-five-plus out of a hundred rated IBM favorably then. Conversely, the following is from Q3 2010:[26]

"I would recommend my company as a great place to work."

Industry comparative responses
- North America IT Industry Best   89%
- North America IT Industry Average   72%

IBM responses
- IBM Worldwide   58%
- IBM Worldwide Software Group   57% (down from 60% in 3Q 2009)
- IBM North America Sales and Distribution 54% (down from 64% in 3Q 2009)
- IBM North America   51% (down from 58% in 1Q 2010)
- IBM Worldwide Systems and Technology Group 50% (down from 55% in 3Q 2009)

When compared to North America's best IT organizations, IBM North America lagged 20 to 38 points behind in the following categories:

- "I would recommend IBM as a great place to work."
- "In IBM, people are rewarded according to their job performance."
- "Even if I were offered a comparable position with similar pay and benefits at another company, I would NOT [emphasis is IBM's] leave IBM."
- "When I do an excellent job, my accomplishments are recognized."
- "IBM is making the changes necessary to compete effectively."
- "Overall, I feel that my career goals can be met at IBM."
- "Processes and procedures allow me to effectively meet my clients' needs."

Over the years, as morale has degraded, IBM's financial leadership has pointed to sales execution as the major problem, but since 2006, IBM's annual reports highlight, ad nauseum, that sales productivity and processes improve every year:

- **2006 IBM Annual Report**—Simplifying and streamlining internal processes has improved operations, sales force productivity and processes, and these actions have improved client satisfaction when working with the company.
- **2007 IBM Annual Report**—Simplifying and streamlining internal processes has improved operations, sales force productivity and processes, and these actions have improved client satisfaction.
- **2008 IBM Annual Report**—Simplifying and streamlining internal processes has improved operations, sales force productivity and processes, and these actions have improved client satisfaction.
- **2009 IBM Annual Report**—Simplifying and streamlining internal processes has improved operations, sales force productivity and processes.
- **2010 IBM Annual Report**—Simplifying and streamlining internal processes has improved operations, sales force productivity and processes.
- **2011 IBM Annual Report**—Simplifying and streamlining internal processes has improved sales force productivity and operational effectiveness and efficiency.

- **2012 IBM Annual Report**—Simplifying and streamlining internal processes has improved sales force productivity and operational effectiveness and efficiency.
- **2013 IBM Annual Report**—Simplifying and streamlining internal processes has improved sales force productivity and operational effectiveness and efficiency.

The historical data (See Fig. 5, p. 105) visually documents the continuing impact of this "simplifying and streamlining" on the IBM sales force over the last twenty years—revenue per employee has been flat since 1994 and fallen 18% since 2004.*

Considering the above, when Rometty pointed to sales execution as the problem in early 2013, what had the corporate leadership been doing for the last eight years? Although revenue per employee can't be the only measure of a healthy corporation, it is the touchstone of how efficiently a company utilizes its sales organization. It is a legitimate cross-industry gauge to measure the success or failure of changes to improve sales productivity.

Even with declining revenue, layoffs can temporarily spike revenue per employee—as evidenced in the early nineties. But a continually growing number is a positive sign. Comparing time periods with equivalent revenue growth in the chart above—58% over the first ten years and 59% percent in the last twenty—revenue per employee, rather than growing an additional 91% in the second period, has been flat or worse. If IBM had matched over the last twenty years the productivity increases of the leading ten years, the actual revenue per employee should have been approximately $400,000 per employee. Would this have been a reasonable expectation for measuring IBM's simplifying and streamlining?

The chart on page 106 (See Fig. 6) documents the 2013 revenue per employee for some major corporations in the IT software, hardware and services industry.

---

* The number of IBM employees used in these calculations is the number of full-time employees and complementary employees (non-wholly owned subsidiary employees).

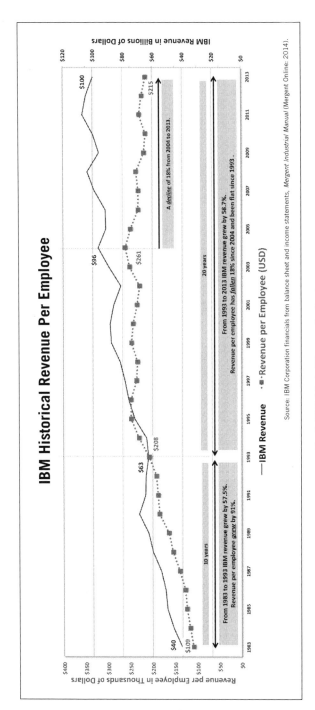

Fig. 5 IBM Historical Revenue Per Employee

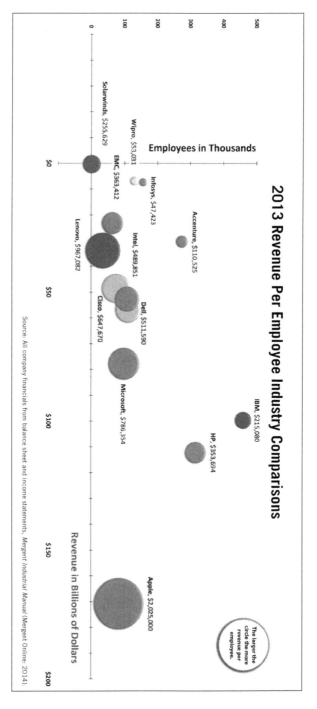

2013 Revenue Per Employee Industry Comparisons

Employees in Thousands

Revenue in Billions of Dollars

Solarwinds, $255,629
Wipro, $53,031
EMC, $363,412
Infosys, $47,423
Accenture, $110,525
Lenovo, $967,082
Intel, $489,851
Dell, $511,590
Cisco, $647,670
Microsoft, $786,354
IBM, $215,080
HP, $353,694
Apple, $2,025,000

The larger the circle the more revenue per employee.

Source: All company financials from balance sheet and income statements, *Mergent Industrial Manual* (Mergent Online: 2014).

Fig. 6 2013 Revenue Per Employee Industry Comparisons

Several of IBM's competitors are easily achieving $500,000 in revenue per employee. IBM should be in the vicinity of them, but even with the economies of scale to its benefit—a larger number of employees and overall revenue—it is not competitive. It has missed an opportunity over the last twenty years to grow with its industry and has instead moved in a negative direction.

When statements like "Processes and procedures allow me to effectively meet my clients' needs" and "IBM's internal processes and policies support the [IBM] values" were put to IBM North America's sales employees, one in three responded favorably; one in three responded negatively; and one in three responded with a shrug of the shoulders. "Processes are effective for customers" was twenty points below the industry average and thirty points behind the industry best.

At the team level, the responses suggest employees are, just as in the 1980s, still trying to put the client first. IBM's processes and procedures are in their way. Put simply, the perspective from those on the customer front lines seems justified—"simplification" and "streamlining" are getting in the way of driving revenue.

I recently interviewed a former IBM product manager who is now at SolarWinds (See Fig. 6, p. 106). We had worked together for several years. He was not laid off. He did not leave for financially greener pastures. He left because of a lack of job satisfaction.

"Pete, I work hard," he said. "You know that. My background is start-ups. I'll work weekdays, weeknights and weekends. No matter where I work, I work this much." He stretched out both his arms. Then he looked at me through a small space between his thumb and forefinger and said, "But at IBM you accomplish this much. At SolarWinds, I work just as hard. The difference is that I make a difference. At IBM, I was paid a six-digit salary to prepare and massage executive charts. How can a motivated person be happy with that? You have no authority; you can't make decisions; yet you are held accountable. No one trusts the individual to make decisions." This point, or something like it, has been brought up in almost every IBM exit interview I have conducted, too.

"You mean Lotus Symphony didn't make you more productive preparing those executive charts?"* We both laughed and went back to our lunch.

We laughed because if IBMers have an up-to-date version of any productivity software — like Microsoft Office — they most likely bought it themselves. I bought all of mine. The most current productivity product an IBMer can get (and most can't) is Microsoft Office 2007. New productivity tools, which often require the latest version of Microsoft Office, rarely interoperate with Lotus Symphony. We spent hours extracting, preparing, inputting, formatting and reformatting information by hand for constant, mind-numbing internal executive reviews.

Increased profits are not coming from streamlining and simplifying but from lower labor costs. They are achieved by shuffling workloads worldwide, avoiding investment and instituting draconian financial restrictions.

But the widening gap between net income and net income per employee since 2004 may indicate that these gains are reaching their limits. (See Fig. 7, p. 109)

And how will IBM India be impacted when this limit is reached? Since IBM hired three to five employees in developing economies to replace one in the United States, they will have to lay off three to five overseas employees to achieve the same financial bottom line effect. In the first quarter of 2009, IBM laid off seventeen thousand employees — most of those in the United States. How many employees will developing economies have to resource to achieve the same "workforce rebalancing"?

More importantly, will employees working in that environment be as dedicated to the company's success as IBMers were in the early nineties? The latest surveys suggest not.

In 2009, IBM dropped from its annual reports that "these actions have improved client satisfaction." Perhaps IBM's executive team is aware that one of its other major stakeholders — its customer base — is also being affected.

---

* IBM Lotus Symphony was a suite of applications for creating, editing and sharing text, spreadsheets and presentations. It was competitive to Microsoft Office and was distributed as freeware until it was discontinued in January 2012.

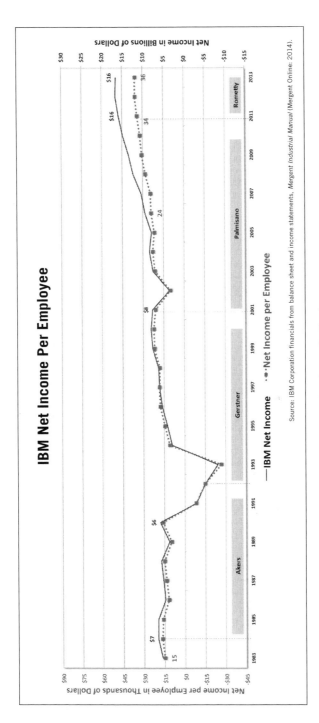

Source: IBM Corporation financials from balance sheet and income statements, *Mergent Industrial Manual* (Mergent Online: 2014).

Fig. 7 IBM Net Income Per Employee

Is the Current Leadership Failing to See Through Their Salesmen's Eyes?

In early 2013 Mark Loughridge, IBM's CFO, stated in an analysts call, "Software growth was impacted by a number of large transactions that rolled into the second quarter."[27] Rometty commented on the same problem, saying, "We were too slow to understand the value and then engage in the approval and the sign-off process—the result? It didn't get done."[28]

Essentially, they were saying "Sales isn't getting it done."

The entire breadth of the IBM client teams used to have excellent industry skills and the depth of customer relationships to get things done. There are still, today, some tremendously skillful IBMers, but the breadth of industry skills and depth of customer understanding have declined. I worked across such industry organizations for years and saw the best in action. They were never slow, and they knew how to engage in a sign-off process.

In January 1998, four of us walked into the IBM New York City branch office. We were meeting with the IBM client executive who owned the relationship with one of America's largest banks. As a software salesman, I had watched, worked and profited from this bank's expansion over the last few years, and we were there to talk about a new software product.

The client executive came in, sat down and put his feet up on the table. He looked at us and said without a second's hesitation, "You either sell me today or you go nowhere with my customer. I own this account. No one, but no one talks to this bank without my permission." It wasn't rehearsed. It had just been repeated once a day, every day for audiences like us over the last twenty years. This was a man from the IBM "old school."

Well, I had several people in the room with me from the old school, too. They could hand it out as well as take it. The senior member, in his "aw, shucks" tone, said, "Tell me three things then. What is the customer's top strategic initiative? If we get your agreement, what is your action plan? What do you bring to the table?"

It was like watching two prizefighters circle the room. They were sizing each other up. This pregnant pause would float until someone finally broke down. I was the showman; they were the sales substance. I knew enough to keep my mouth shut.

Finally, the IBM client executive smiled and said, "Let me take them in reverse order. What do I bring to the table? The CIO is the decision maker. We have known each other since the founding of this bank. Our wives knit together. Our children go to the same school. We go to sports games together. I own the IBM relationship. I have access. I care about this customer more than anyone else in this company.

"What is the action plan? If you get that far, you will go through another presentation with the full IBM team. It will require you to revisit the customer over and over again this year. You will start with the lower level departments and work your way up. You will listen and adapt your plans after every meeting to address each department's objections and requirements. It will end with a final, single presentation to the chief information officer with all his direct reports. If you do your job right, that final meeting will just be a formality."

He stopped to look around the room. This guy was full of himself, but as we say in Texas, "If it's fact, it ain't braggin'."

He continued, "What is the customer's top strategic play? My technical guys tell me your product fits within the bank's 'Branch of the Future' project. You would not have gotten my attention if my technical guys hadn't given it a thumbs-up."

Then he tapped on the table to get everyone's attention. "And finally, this deal will not close until the end of the year. Do not tell anyone otherwise. Sometime in late December, I will have dinner with the bank's CIO. We will call IBM Software Group's general manager, get an extra discount and sign the deal."

He stood up to refill his coffee and said with his back to us, "If you are included in the deal, and that is still questionable, you will have earned your commission checks. They will arrive in January." He turned around, sat down, placed his coffee on the table and asked, "Can we get started now?"

True to his word, the largest software deal in IBM history closed in December, and since we had proven the value of our software to the customer, our commission checks arrived a month later. The client executive executed flawlessly: he owned the customer relationship; he held their trust and confidence because of a lifetime of personal interactions; and he had access to decision makers. On the back end he drove the IBM machine to meet his customer's requirements; he worked and reworked, adjusted and readjusted, aligned and realigned expectations to close a deal.

He was the epitome of independent thought and action; he didn't brag, he just stated the facts.

He left IBM later that year.

It Is About Human Relations

When large deals slip, it *is* the most troubling of sales problems. It is a relationship problem; and the solution will not be found in the timely return of phone calls. The heart of the problem is the internal processes that damage human capital, destroy sales force morale and impact client satisfaction.

Growth only comes through a corporation's employee-owners, and long-term profit is only found in a customer-driven product portfolio — not an earnings-driven one. The relentless pounding of indiscriminant resource actions at best demoralizes the many and at worst drives away the best and brightest; and the financial system supports products of no value that are at best a distraction and at worst destroying customer relationships.

IBM's salesman-in-chief once achieved growth by seeing a human being as a relationship, not a resource. He conducted Family Days that were the twentieth century's "Relationship Action Days."

This family once sought growth together.

Endnotes

1 Peter E. Greulich, *The World's Greatest Salesman* (MBI Concepts Corporation, Austin, Texas, 2011), p. 257.

2 Louis V. Gerstner, Jr., *Who Says Elephants Can't Dance?* (Harper Business, New York, 2002), p. 22.

3 Steve Lohr, "IBM Chief Making Drastic New Cuts," *New York Times*, July 28, 1993.

4 "IBM Q1 2013 Earnings Call Transcript," Morningstar, April 19, 2013.

5 IBM e-mail to IBMers from Chairman, President and Chief Executive Officer, subject: Fourth-Quarter, Full-Year 2008 Earnings, January 20, 2009.

6 Sam Palmisano, chairman, president and CEO, IBM Intranet Web posting, January 20 2009.

7 *Austin American* staff, "IBM Begins Layoffs: Austin Impact Unclear," *Austin American-Statesman*, January 21, 2009.

8 IBM e-mail to all Tivoli employees from Tivoli general manager, subject: Tivoli 4Q08 Results, January 22 2009.

9 IBM e-mail to all Tivoli employees from Software Group senior vice president, subject: SWG 4Q 2008 Performance, January 22, 2009.

10 Thomas J. Watson Sr., *Men — Minutes — Money* (IBM Corporation, New York, 1934), p. 104, reprinted with permission of IBM.

11 Although it was not publicly disclosed, several articles document the price at $46 million. One of these being Joanne van Erp Montague and Davis Wright Tremaine LLP, *Copyright Issues with Open Source Software* (Davis Wright Tremaine LLP, 2011), p. 11.

12 Terrence Cosgrove and Ronni J. Colville, *Magic Quadrant for PC Life Cycle Configuration Management, 2007* (Gartner RAS Core Research Note G00153428, 21 December 2007), p. 5.

13 Katie Hoffmann and Serena Saitto, "IBM to Buy BigFix for About $400 Million to Add Security Software Products," *Bloomberg Technology*, July 1, 2010.

14 IBM press release, "IBM Forms New Watson Group," January 9, 2014.

15 IBM press release, "IBM Commits $1 Billion to Fuel Linux," September 17, 2013.

16 IBM press release, "IBM Commits $1.2 Billion to Expand Global Cloud Footprint," January 17, 2014.

17 IBM press release, "IBM Drives Flash Technology," September 17, 2013.

18 Sarah Frier, "IBM Bets $1 Billion on New Mainframe," *Bloomberg Technology*, August 28, 2012.

19 IBM press release, "IBM Sets the Stage for the Next Era of Computing," April 11, 2012.

20 IBM press release, "IBM to Acquire Kenexa to Bolster Social Business Initiatives," August 12, 2012.

21 IBM press release, "IBM Makes $4 Billion in Financing Available for Business Partners," November 15, 2012.

22 Doug Henschen, "IBM Plans Layoffs, New Investments," *InformationWeek*, January 22, 2014.

23 Jim Collins, *Built to Last* (HarperCollins Publishers Inc., New York, 1994) and *Good to Great* (HarperCollins Publishers Inc., New York, 2001).

24 Thomas J. Watson Jr., *Thirty Years of Management Briefings* (IBM Corporation, Armonk, New York, 1988), reprinted with permission of IBM.

25 Samuel J. Palmisano, *2010 Corporate Responsibility Summary*, May 2011.

26 *IBM Pulse and Values Survey Report*, North America Total, 3Q 2010.

27 Morningstar, International Business Machines, Q1 2013 Earnings Call Transcript.

28 "IBM's Chief to Employees: Think Fast, Move Faster," *Wall Street Journal*, April 24, 2013.

CHAPTER SIX

REIGNITING A TRUE BLUE DÉJÀ VU

> ❝ Nobody can see except from his [or her] own point of view; and the executive's angle of vision must be a narrow one for him [or her] to be effective. The fact that other people in other positions have another point of view may not only escape the corporation executive, it may even be incomprehensible to him [or her]. What is needed is not "facts" but an ability to see facts as others see them."[1]
>
> **Peter F. Drucker**, *The Concept of the Corporation*

Understanding IBM's Economic Engine

IBM analysts offer varying views on IBM's future. Most are short-term economic weather forecasts that evaluate what is on the surface. They see the immediate and overwhelming threats—the ones that can be seen, heard or felt. And they forecast growth. On the surface it would appear to be déjà vu.

But it is different this time. For a century, Big Blue's colossal cultural currents have swelled, billowed and rumbled ever onward. Change here is imperceptible except over extended periods of time—exactly the perspective that eludes human awareness and rational discussion. And these currents are changing course.

Perhaps only a Watson-trained financial mind would see storms on the horizon for the company in the chart. (See Fig. 8, p.117) But this is the direction the company is headed in thanks to the changes of the last thirty years.

Bringing these changes into focus is unpleasant, but in understanding them rests the true story of IBM's first hundred years, and the key to the company finding its way in the second.

Dale Carnegie wrote, "A man convinced against his will is of the same opinion still." IBM's twenty-first-century leadership is of a singularly financial mind, and there's no easy way to convince this financial mind that culture was once its economic engine. The financial mind desires quantifiable data—to divide the cost of gas by the miles driven and then ask if the driver took the shortest route. It doesn't comprehend a driving force that keeps a corporation running past empty—the explanation for such a corporation would be dismissed as nothing more than a myth.

You can't plug myths into a spreadsheet, but to those who understand human nature, it is as simple as the difference between seeking shelter in a corporate house and building a corporate home. I know that the distinction between the words "house" and "home" will not translate easily across the 175 countries that comprise IBM, so here's another exercise in imagination to steel the wills of those who desire to build a corporate home and help the financial minds to find in their spreadsheets an entry labeled "character."

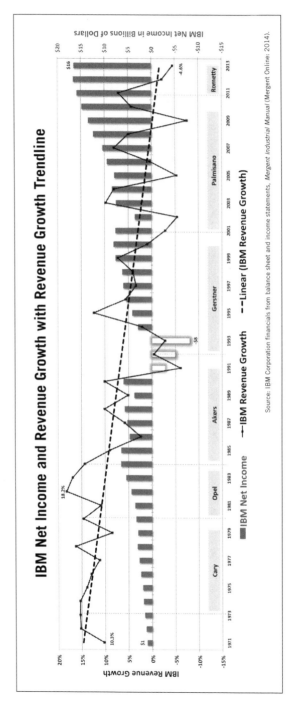

Fig. 8 IBM Net Income and Revenue Growth with Revenue Growth Trendline

Imagine a fire that flares up between two family structures. With both houses ablaze, a single male occupant escapes from each, and the two find each other on their front lawns, waiting for the fire trucks to arrive.

Both of their families are out of town for the weekend. They agree they are very fortunate. Temporarily frozen somewhere between relief and fear, they are glad that their families' lives were not at stake, yet terrified by the devastation glaring intently down on them.

One of them lowers himself stiffly with his arm onto the recently manicured lawn. He mumbles about not having "time for this." With school just starting, it would be a nightmare replacing this rental house.

But as the second man — we'll call him Jim — watches a small section of his roof collapse, a wide swath of light brings his nightmare into focus. He senses for the first time what he is about to lose.

Shaken awake, he realizes that the firefighters will take too long. He sprints into the blaze.

He goes first into the family room, grabbing a cumbersome family album — a thick, tattered, torn and worn assemblage of pictures. He emerges from the front door clutching it against his chest, keeping his body between it and the fire that reaches out from above and behind. Pictures dangle out from every edge. When he drops the album on the lawn, photos scatter everywhere. A growing crowd sees his family memories unfold in the flickering light: a young newlywed couple, first-born through last-born child, now older children tickling children of their own, grandparents becoming great-grandparents, and now a retired husband and spouse in faraway lands.

As he turns for another desperate dash, Jim sees the fire's backdraft tugging at the loose pictures, pulling them end-over-end back to it across the lawn. He hesitates. Does he save a few pictures or does he push again into the fire for the next precious item? A sudden updraft flips over one large portrait — the last picture taken of his whole family. He has bent over to press it against the ground, hoping to hold it in place, when a young woman, sensing his dilemma, steps forward from the crowd. In the midst of the hysteria she herself is a picture — of calm and composure. She touches his shoulder and reaches to gather up the stately family portrait. Jim's eyes show gratitude before turning again toward the burning building.

As he sprints forward, he glances up into the second-floor master bedroom. The crowd stands in hushed silence as they watch what they think is a man bent on self-destruction.

Someone in the back yells, "I see him upstairs!" People raise their hands over their eyes. Jim *is* on the second floor.

They squint in vain to peer through the smoke and fire for a glimpse of their neighbor deep in the building. The emotions in the crowd range from incredulity to fascination to wonderment to fear to understanding to desperation. Yet he emerges again with more precious cargo: a framed, faded drawing of two stick parents with a stick child between; a delicate papier-mâché handprint freezing innocence in time; a tapestry frantically ripped from the master bedroom wall—the only memento his wife of thirty years ever bought impulsively. He knows its value to her, but if she were here, she would catch his attention with a tender whisper: "We can always go to Belgium again." To be sure he really heard, she would plead, "What is most important to me is 'we.' "

But she's not there and Jim is desperate. He's determined to risk his life one more time—a last attempt to feel his way into the three smaller bedrooms. He wants to gather a single item from each—one timeless gem for each of his children. For thirty years, many times in the dark of night, he's lived in these rooms: at first it was endlessly rocking a sick child while memorizing the placement and curve of each artifact (what else was there to do during such times?); later in their lives, he would just stand quietly watching them sleep, realizing how blessed he was; now, late in his life, he often sits on the edges of their empty beds awash in memories. He doesn't need to see; he can find every item on his unwritten list by touch.

In a moment of clarity he sees the young woman again. She's saved the pictures from the fire. She's gathered them together. She's placed them carefully back into the album. He watches as she smoothes the last picture on the last page into place. Then she slowly closes the album on his life.

He turns to look deep into the fire. His neighbors scream for him to stop, but his personal fire burns so deep and so hot it will never let go. As he thinks of all he's losing, a shadow moves between him and his last pursuit. He welcomes it—this personal harbinger of death. He bolts forward and taunts it to accompany him back into the fire.

An experienced fire chief arriving on the scene knows instantly that both these structures are lost. His job now is to intercept emotion long enough for sanity and common sense to return. He looks first for the homeowners—the ones watching their memories disappear in smoke. These are the ones reacting out of instinct and disregard for their own safety. He's seen overwhelming despair drive many to the very edges of sanity's abyss, and this man standing before him the old fire chief knows well. The chief stands strong—a lone silhouette between the fire and the bedraggled, frantic man bent on self-destruction. The old fire chief is a shadow, but he's the shadow of life.

The owner halts for a moment, stares right at the old fireman and rushes forward. He grabs the chief by the arm and screams, begs him to come with him into the burning building.

With a caring firmness, the chief catches his shoulder and pulls him to the ground. He restrains him from what would have been his last effort, for the building is on the verge of complete collapse. Water from the fire trucks pours through gaping holes in the roof. Jim's last precious possessions disappear.

As the homeowner realizes he is helpless to do more, he falls still. He's spent. The old fireman, sensing the man's resignation, relaxes his grip, knowing that overwhelming grief will now pin Jim to the ground.

The fire burns so hot that many standing nearby retreat. Yet the fire chief remains with his ward. More firemen, realizing the lost cause, silently form a semicircle with their heavy suits to shield the two men from the oppressive heat. In this protected place the young woman returns. She rests the album in the man's hands. It's time for her to return to her home, stand quietly in her daughter's bedroom and weep.

As she moves into the crowd, she brushes past a small child. Even more than the adults, this innocent senses the suffering of this distraught man. Holding her mother's hand, she whispers, "Mommy, why did he keep going back into the house?"

He overhears her and turns. The embarrassed mother instinctively pulls her daughter closer, but Jim says gently, "This is the place where my first and my last child were born. This is where, for thirty years, I broke bread with my friends and celebrated so many Thanksgivings that I would forget most of them except for these pictures." With his thumb he wipes black ash from a long-deceased friend's face. "I consoled family and friends here. On the shelves in the living room are...were the pictures of our lives. Stored in our attic were memories so precious, I can't comprehend trying to remember them all. This was my home."

His neighbor, meanwhile, is on the phone with a property manager. There's another house for rent just up the street. He can move in next week.

IBM Was Home

Since 1914, IBMers have returned over and over again to save their corporate home. Such a simple concept confounds the cynical, yet this is what powered the twentieth century's most adaptable economic engine. The Watsons understood its power, and their culture was a gift to any CEO humble enough to accept it.

Tom Watson Jr., late in his life, reached out personally to Mr. Gerstner. We are privy only to the few words documented in *Who Says Elephants Can't Dance?*:

> A special moment occurred during those first weeks of April. I walked out of my home one morning at my usual early hour. However, when I opened my car door, I suddenly realized there was someone sitting in the back seat. It was Thomas J. Watson, Jr.... He was 79 years old, and he had retired as CEO of IBM in 1971. He was animated and perhaps better stated, agitated. He said he was angry about what had happened to "my company."[2]

"My company," indeed.

If Watson Jr. could ride one more time in the company of his twenty-first-century counterparts, he would again express anger over what has happened to "my company." Only this time, he would linger a little longer to ensure he was really understood. He would add, "What is important to me is 'we.' "

IBM's strength was always in "us."

Employee-Owners Overcome Their Blindness

There is a folktale that some give a Chinese origin, but it seems to be told almost anyplace where there are elephants. As the story goes, three blind men are discussing a new animal they heard about in the market — the elephant. Hearing stories of its wonderful feats, they wish they could touch one.

It so happens, that a passing merchant overhears them.

"The elephant is how we carry our goods," he tells them. "Come with me."

Happily, they follow him — discussing the whole way how they might experience this new beast.

When they get to the merchant's campsite, he tells the men that he must, for their safety, take them sep-

> **An IBM Employee-Owner**
>
> There is a term used to describe the men and women who call IBM home: IBMer. I have never discovered any stories or corporate mythology as to the origin of the term, but it came to describe employees who made business decisions as if they carried the owner's burden.
>
> Being an IBMer was not about stock options, social class, corporate hierarchy, educational stature, pay grade or time-in-service; rather it described a person of commitment, dedication and loyalty. It was an individual in a win-win relationship with his company and part of a corporate family. There were leaders but we discussed issues as peers, united around achieving a common goal — the topic of this book.

arately. He cannot have all three so close to the elephant at the same time.

So he leads the first blind man to the elephant and places the man's hands on its trunk. After that he leads the second man forward and lets him feel a powerful leg. Finally he leads the last man forward, who laughs as the elephant's tail whisks over him.

When they are done, the blind men thank the merchant profusely. They are all amazed and rush off so they can discuss this new experience.

As they sit, the first man can barely control himself. "It is like a huge snake, but much stronger."

"No, it was strong but solid," the second man says. "It did not twist. It had a base like a huge tree."

The third man questions both of them. "My elephant was like a wispy fan."

To this day, they argue. Of course, the moral is "Can anyone describe the whole unless he understands all the parts?"

When all the powers of the office would seem to ensure a limitless view, it must be hard for a CEO to accept that her perspective may be obscured. She has the authority, the access and the ability to gather information simply by commenting on her need for it. Junior executives, managers, staff and consultants line up before her for their moment in the sun. But she must be ever on her guard, watching for advisors who say what is easy to hear rather than what needs to be heard, for counselors who place blame rather than accept it, for predecessors concerned with their legacy rather than the business, and for electronic surveys of employee thoughts that cannot replace hearing them herself.

If the CEO asks her elephant to dance, it is a certainty that it will be made to do so, but should it? Who would tell her otherwise?

Unlike the CEO, it is easy for an employee to recognize his or her limited perspective. As the employee labors beneath the beast, he or she may see little that is wondrous in a dancing elephant. To the employee it is scary and unpredictable. It dances atop friends' livelihoods. It toys with the employee's ability to spend a little, save a little and retire away from the thundering herd. It can, in an instant, destroy the employee. He or she knows that nimbleness is required and adapts, yet sees even the most nimble of friends crushed. The employee feels the elephant's suffering, but what the employee once loved is now feared.

With such a limited perspective, how can there be any value in the employee's perspective? Who can he tell?

While the executive's view may be fraught with misperceptions, generalizations and isolation, the employee's view may be myopic, superficial and limited, and either may be swayed by greed. No matter the position, to gain an expansive view requires communication, openness, patience and humility. It requires becoming an employee-owner.

An employee-owner — whether atop or beneath the elephant — changes positions to gain perspective. He or she shares new insights clearly and unselfishly so that others will learn. For a lifetime these employee-owners discuss their elephant's every movement and nurse its every wound. They establish a rhythm of life with it and never allow another caretaker to threaten its well-being. Their intuition is honed to recognize their ward's slightest movement in fear or distress; and they learn to calm it — with a light touch on a tender spot in its rough hide. These employee-owners are the elephant's true caretakers — blind men that overcame their limitations to become the wisest of counselors.

And the truth is we are all blind.

An Ideal Continuation of Tradition – The Path to Growth

IBM needs a salesman-in-chief to restore balance. It takes a salesman-in-chief to sell her customers only products of value, and it takes a salesman-in-chief to retain top-notch salesmen — entrepreneurs who maintain strong relationships by living in their customers' realities.

For IBM to grow again Ms. Rometty needs 463,785 employee-owners to wake up each day enthusiastic about growing their business. IBM achieved its 2010 Road Map. But before he left, Palmisano set in stone the 2015 Road Map for his successor, and although it will not be achieved early, it will be achieved. Presumably, there are financial wizards already thinking about 2020.

Even to the shortsighted, these road maps are dangerous paths. It is hard to say who believes in them, but it is definitely not the majority Rometty needs to grow the business.

Many say that IBM is too large. That it has peaked, and the strategies driving these road maps must now be optimization of profits, remaining a financial organization and managing the stock price. IBM's founder faced a similar situation with C-T-R a century earlier. He made his decision, and it kept IBM growing for almost eight decades. If anyone understood all the parts of the IBM business it was the founders.

And their road map? A business that would go on forever.

On the restaurant menu at Austria's famous Hotel Sacher are the words "Everything that is new is usually nothing but the promising child of time-tested older achievements—an ideal continuation of tradition." If so, then the road map to the future for IBM is in the time-tested traditions of Tom Watson Sr. and his son. The success of those traditions was in their simplicity. They enabled IBM to reach the doorstep of the twenty-first century.

IBM's Corporate Constitution created a monopoly through the twentieth century—though it was a monopoly on culture, not computers, and no government ever named it in an antitrust suit. Every corporation sought employees who exhibited independent thought and action in alignment with its goals; yet few implemented the means to achieve that end. IBM achieved it, but then discarded it as an irrelevant remnant of the past. As a result, growth stalled, and IBM has been searching ever since to replace the simplicity of three words. Lou Gerstner discussed eight principles, which covered two pages in his book. Palmisano replaced Gerstner's principles with five traits and nine competencies, which take up several Web pages. No IBMer of today can tell you what is on those Web pages; but 100% of the Watsons' IBMers knew Respect, Service and Excellence, and everyone exhibited all three. After all, everything they really needed to know they learned in kindergarten, and IBM just extended society's most basic building blocks.

Only a constitution can ensure right over might, build trust and confidence and be a corporate compass in the roughest of economic terrain. It calls mankind to True Service and ensures that a company is willing to change everything about itself except its core values and most fundamental of beliefs. A constitution holds a leader accountable. Only a constitution can legitimize leadership and make all employee-owners peers to eliminate the elephant in the room.

Respect will never be found in 140 characters. Earning Respect takes time, personal closeness and character. Respect is the self-pruning mechanism that removes those who lack the desire or ability to perform. Respect legitimizes leadership. It enables a decentralized organization to function without departmental dictatorships or anarchy. Respect calls all people from all walks of life. It is Respect that ensures a corporation's diversity of thought, temperament and ideas. Respect is always about the individual.

Service sets the right objective to support gracious self-sacrifice. True Service must be modeled by the leadership and expected from every employee-owner. Service calls men and women to be part of something greater. Service builds a family spirit that creates a sustainable corporate culture. Service delivers that renewable source of human energy every business needs to go on forever. In a capitalistic society, Service distributes profits equitably between the four investors in a corporation — customers, shareholders, employees and society. It is in True Service that a family forms bonds and a house transforms into a home.

Excellence is the agent of change. Excellence seeks out the best path. Excellence is the champion of the wild duck — those who won't be tamed or shamed into being company men. Excellence understands that profit is in the relationship not the product, and that long-term growth is in a better planet not necessarily a "smarter" one. In the darkest of times, it forgives thoughtful mistakes to drive invention and innovation. Excellence is the goal ever pursued yet never achieved.

This constitution encourages individual thought and emboldens individual action.

It is the ideal continuation of the Watsons' tradition.

What Does the Twenty-First Century Hold?

Tom Watson Jr., in a lecture at the Columbia Graduate School of Business in 1962, discussed IBM's Basic Beliefs. He said that these beliefs weren't the only ones for business.

He was being too humble. If he had been in Philadelphia in 1787, I believe he would have fought for the U.S. Constitution to be framed around the same three words. "Everything else," he would have said, "should be left to future generations to change, evolve and rewrite."

He speculated as to the cause of the decline of a corporation: technology, changing tastes, fashions? He ruled these out. He reviewed the common wisdom of his day on the cause: business competence, market judgment and quality of leadership. He ruled these vital but not decisive.

Rather, he said:

> I believe the real difference between success and failure in a corporation can very often be traced to the question of how well the organization brings out the great energies and talents of its people. What does it do to help these people find common cause with each other? How does it keep them pointed in the right direction despite the many rivalries and differences which may exist among them? And how can it sustain this common cause and sense of direction through the many changes which take place from one generation to another?[3]

IBM understood the answers to these questions once. Its future lies in their rediscovery.

Endnotes

1 Peter F. Drucker, *The Concept of the Corporation* (New American Library, 1964), p. 82.

2 Louis V. Gerstner, Jr., *Who Says Elephants Can't Dance?* (Harper Business, New York 2002), p. 37.

3 Thomas J. Watson Jr., *A Business and Its Beliefs* (McGraw-Hill Book Company, Inc., New York, Toronto, London, 1963), p. 19.

AFTERWORD

> **❝** No one, it is true, can look ahead and foretell with un-failing accuracy what the future will bring, but that is not necessary, for just as historians judge the past in the light of the present, we can envision the future out of our knowledge of what has taken place in the past and what is going on about us now.**❞**
>
> **Thomas J. Watson Sr.**, speaking on the Earmarks of a Business Man.

Elephants in Braille

Two artists have invited you into their shared gallery. You expected to see two separate works on display but are puzzled because all you see is a single block of black granite—almost twelve feet wide by six feet deep and reaching a misshapen twenty-four feet high.

"Stop here," the first artist says. "My masterpiece must be viewed from afar."

You move from one side of the rock to the other—left, right and back again. As you fix your gaze on the stone's face, shadows appear. You tilt your head from side to side, but the image remains hidden. Then you climb a high platform and look down. From here, a wondrous animal—etched in low relief—emerges from the reflective surface of the dense monolith. Shadows outline a wonderful beast, and its many exquisite features come into focus: ears emerge from the cold stone, eyes fill with expression, and a trunk is raised high as it rears up on two powerful back legs as if in a victory dance. This elephant as you study it—so far, only from a distance—demands closer study.

As you move forward—leaving the first artist behind—the second greets you.

"When you are ready, touch it," he says.

You place your hand on the elephant. There are thousands of individual dots, each varying in height and texture. They vary in width; some are flat; some are pleasantly blunt and others sharp. You let your fingers ride across the rough hide and slide across small sections of smooth skin. There are hundreds of thousands of miniscule monoliths composing this single megalithic scene of a dancing elephant on the face of a magnificent menhir.

"It is Braille interweaved within the composition of the granite," the artist says.

Your fingers overhear stories of true service, right over might, and self-sacrifice; but they also tell of the appearance of an ever-present, ever-watchful and seemingly always-ominous elephant in the room.

"But which of these works is true—far or near?" you ask.

"I have never seen an elephant dance," the second artist replies. "I am blind.

"And my colleague has never felt the stories."

Two men in two books have described two different entries into IBM's twenty-first century. One, sitting atop, saw it dance; the other, from beneath, felt the reappearance of the elephant in the room. Two authors have used words to convey their perceptions of the same corporate history—two artists have asked you to evaluate their works of art.

Now you must analyze, assimilate and make your own judgment.

Think and act.

IBM CEO INFORMATION

As discussed in the preface, my initial study concerned IBM's cultural changes. As I continued studying IBM and its leadership, I also started looking at the economic and historical environments in which each of its leaders managed.

Some of the charts in this appendix — e.g., "Largest Declines in U.S. Stock Market History" and "United States Business Cycle Contractions and Expansions"— have been referenced within the text of this book and are complete. Others—e.g., "IBM Historical Revenue Growth" and "Stockholder Return on Investment"—are just an initial sample of the information being consolidated on IBM's one-hundred-year history. These charts were not used in the text of this book as further work needs to be done to improve on their accuracy. If you find them useful, would like to discuss the information, find errors or have suggestions on improvements, contact info@mbiconcepts.com.

Largest Declines in U.S. Stock Market History*

Chief Executive Officer	Number of Stock Market Declines	1910	1920	1930	1940	1950	1960	1970	1980	1990	2000	2010
Thomas J. Watson Sr.	4	#4	#1	#5	#6							
Thomas J. Watson Jr.	2						#12	#7				
T. Vincent Learson	Partial							#3				
Frank T. Cary	1							#3				
John R. Opel	0											
John F. Akers	1								#10			
Louis V. Gerstner	Partial									#2		
Samuel J. Palmisano	1										#2	
Virginia M. Rometty	0											

Rank	Event Description
#1	Crash of 1929, First Part of the Great Depression
#2	Dot-com Bubble Burst (00–02), Crash of 07–09
#3	Inflationary Bear Market, Vietnam, Watergate
#4	World War I, Postwar Auto Bubble Burst
#5	Second Part of Great Depression, World War II
#6	Postwar World War II Bear Market
#7	Start of Inflationary Bear Market
#10	Black Monday–October 19, 1987
#12	Height of the Cold War, Cuban Missile Crisis

CEO tenure

Stock Market Length of Decline
Stock Market Historical Ranking   # Rank

* Stock market declines do not necessarily align with National Bureau of Economic Research, Inc., recessions.
Source: © 2013 Morningstar. All rights reserved. Used with permission. From Morningstar 2013 Ibbotson Stocks, Bonds, Bills, and Inflation (SBBI) Classic Yearbook. Morningstar's 2013 Ibbotson SBBI Classic Yearbook documents the largest U.S. stock market declines exceeding 20% from January 1871 to December 2012. We have only included those applicable during our time frame.

United States Business Cycle Contractions*

Chief Executive Officer	Number of Economic Downturns	1910	1920	1930	1940	1950	1960	1970	1980	1990	2000	2010
Thomas J. Watson Sr.	10											
Thomas J. Watson Jr.	3											
T. Vincent Learson	0											
Frank T. Cary	2											
John R. Opel	1											
John F. Akers	1											
Louis V. Gerstner	1											
Samuel J. Palmisano	1											
Virginia M. Rometty	0											

CEO tenure

Recession (Length of contraction)

The Great Depression

(< 12 months)

(12 to 24 months)

(43 months)

* Source: National Bureau of Economic Research, Inc. Contractions start at the peak of a business cycle and end at the trough.

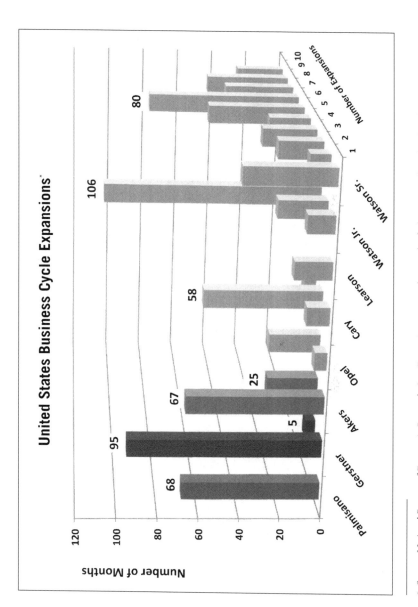

United States Business Cycle Expansions*

Number of Months

* Source: National Bureau of Economic Research, Inc. Expansions start at the trough of a business cycle and end at the peak.

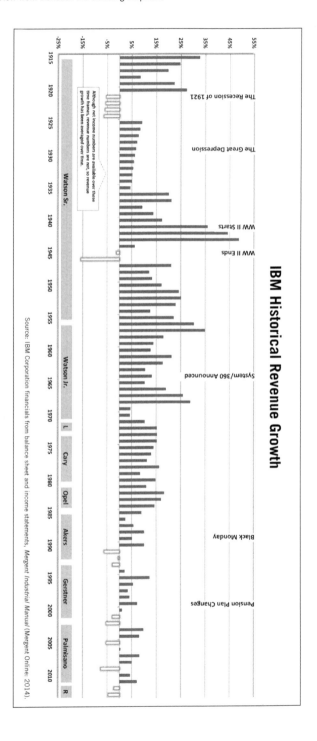

IBM Historical Revenue Growth

Stockholder Return on Investment[*]

Thomas J. Watson Sr. – Growth of $1,000

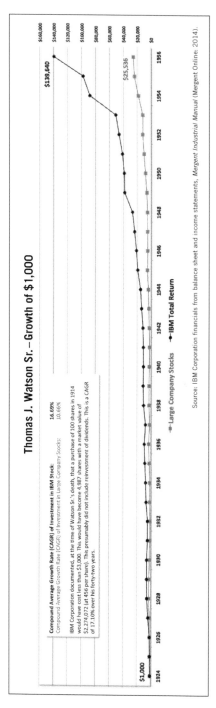

Compound Average Growth Rate (CAGR) of Investment in IBM Stock:	**16.69%**
Compound Average Growth Rate (CAGR) of Investment in Large Company Stocks:	10.66%

IBM Corporation documented, at the time of Watson Sr.'s death, that a purchase of 100 shares in 1914 would have cost less than $3,000. This would have become 4,987 shares with a market value of $2,274,072 (at 456 per share). This presumably did not include reinvestment of dividends. This is a CAGR of 17.10% over his forty-two years.

$139,640

$25,536

— Large Company Stocks **— IBM Total Return**

Source: IBM Corporation financials from balance sheet and income statements, *Mergent Industrial Manual* (Mergent Online: 2014).

Stockholder Return on Investment*

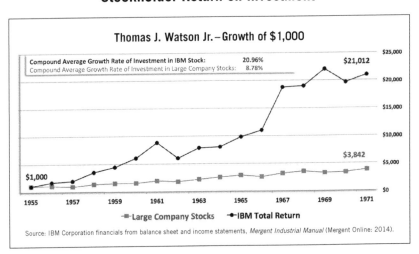

Source: IBM Corporation financials from balance sheet and income statements, *Mergent Industrial Manual* (Mergent Online: 2014).

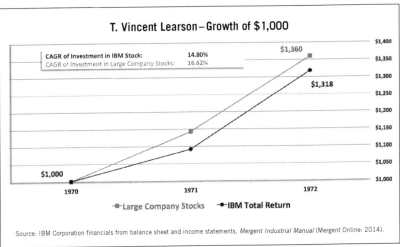

Source: IBM Corporation financials from balance sheet and income statements, *Mergent Industrial Manual* (Mergent Online: 2014).

---

* Source for Large Company Stocks: Total Returns: © 2013 Morningstar. All rights reserved.
Used with permission. *From Morningstar 2013 Ibbotson SBBI Classic Yearbook.*
IBM returns include capital appreciation and income returns without reinvestment of dividends.

Stockholder Return on Investment*

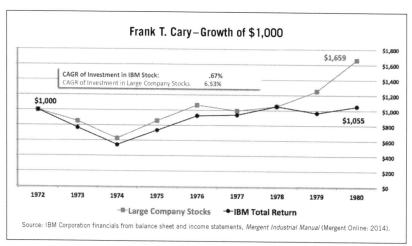

Frank T. Cary–Growth of $1,000

CAGR of Investment in IBM Stock: .67%
CAGR of Investment in Large Company Stocks 6.53%

$1,000

$1,659

$1,055

| $1,800 |
| $1,600 |
| $1,400 |
| $1,200 |
| $1,000 |
| $800 |
| $600 |
| $400 |
| $200 |
| $0 |

1972 1973 1974 1975 1976 1977 1978 1979 1980

–■–Large Company Stocks ─♦─IBM Total Return

Source: IBM Corporation financials from balance sheet and income statements, *Mergent Industrial Manual* (Mergent Online: 2014).

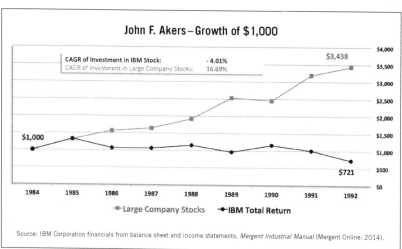

John F. Akers–Growth of $1,000

CAGR of Investment in IBM Stock: - 4.01%
CAGR of Investment in Large Company Stocks: 16.69%

$3,438

$1,000

$721

| $4,000 |
| $3,500 |
| $3,000 |
| $2,500 |
| $2,000 |
| $1,500 |
| $1,000 |
| $500 |
| $0 |

1984 1985 1986 1987 1988 1989 1990 1991 1992

–■–Large Company Stocks ─♦─IBM Total Return

Source: IBM Corporation financials from balance sheet and income statements, *Mergent Industrial Manual* (Mergent Online: 2014).

---

* Source for Large Company Stocks: Total Returns: © 2013 Morningstar. All rights reserved.
Used with permission. *From Morningstar 2013 Ibbotson SBBI Classic Yearbook.*
IBM returns include capital appreciation and income returns without reinvestment of dividends.

Stockholder Return on Investment*

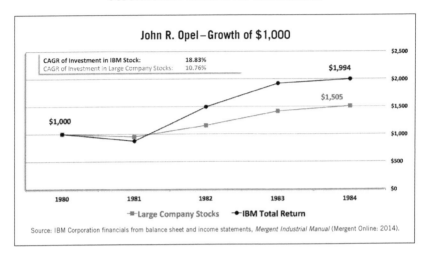

John R. Opel – Growth of $1,000

| CAGR of Investment in IBM Stock: | 18.83% |
| CAGR of Investment in Large Company Stocks: | 10.76% |

$1,994

$1,505

$1,000

- ■ - Large Company Stocks   — ◆ — IBM Total Return

Source: IBM Corporation financials from balance sheet and income statements, *Mergent Industrial Manual* (Mergent Online: 2014).

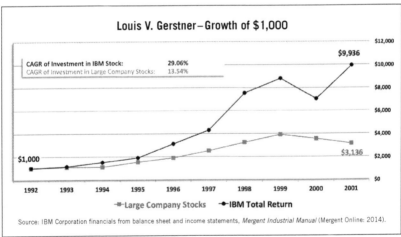

Louis V. Gerstner – Growth of $1,000

| CAGR of Investment in IBM Stock: | 29.06% |
| CAGR of Investment in Large Company Stocks: | 13.54% |

$9,936

$3,136

$1,000

- ■ - Large Company Stocks   — ◆ — IBM Total Return

Source: IBM Corporation financials from balance sheet and income statements, *Mergent Industrial Manual* (Mergent Online: 2014).

---

* Source for Large Company Stocks: Total Returns: © 2013 Morningstar. All rights reserved. Used with permission. *From Morningstar 2013 Ibbotson SBBI Classic Yearbook.*
IBM returns include capital appreciation and income returns without reinvestment of dividends.

Stockholder Return on Investment*

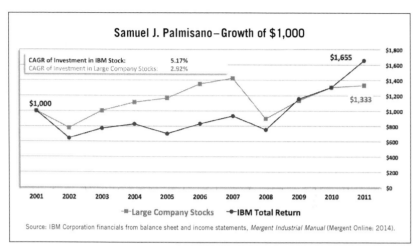

Samuel J. Palmisano – Growth of $1,000

CAGR of Investment in IBM Stock: 5.17%
CAGR of Investment in Large Company Stocks: 2.92%

$1,000

$1,655

$1,333

$1,800
$1,600
$1,400
$1,200
$1,000
$800
$600
$400
$200
$0

2001 2002 2003 2004 2005 2006 2007 2008 2009 2010 2011

Large Company Stocks   IBM Total Return

Source: IBM Corporation financials from balance sheet and income statements, *Mergent Industrial Manual* (Mergent Online: 2014).

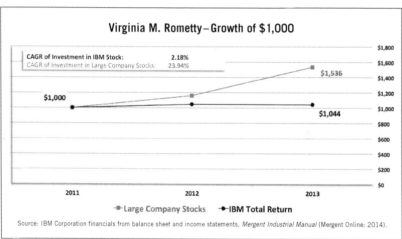

Virginia M. Rometty – Growth of $1,000

CAGR of Investment in IBM Stock: 2.18%
CAGR of Investment in Large Company Stocks: 23.94%

$1,000

$1,536

$1,044

$1,800
$1,600
$1,400
$1,200
$1,000
$800
$600
$400
$200
$0

2011 2012 2013

Large Company Stocks   IBM Total Return

Source: IBM Corporation financials from balance sheet and income statements, *Mergent Industrial Manual* (Mergent Online: 2014).

* Source for Large Company Stocks: Total Returns: © 2013 Morningstar. All rights reserved.
Used with permission. *From Morningstar 2013 Ibbotson SBBI Classic Yearbook.*
IBM returns include capital appreciation and income returns without reinvestment of dividends.

HISTORY OF NATIONAL CASH REGISTER (NCR) SHERMAN ANTITRUST TRIAL

> ❝ Reputation is what people think you are; character is what you really are; what you know yourself to be. ❞
>
> **Thomas J. Watson Sr.**

Jan 1912	It is estimated that NCR controls 95% of cash register market.
Feb 22, 1912	John H. Patterson as CEO, Thomas J. Watson as sales manager and twenty-eight others are indicted for violation of Sherman Antitrust Act.
Nov 19, 1912	Defendants plead not guilty. Jury selection begins.
Feb 13, 1913	Verdict is announced at U.S. District Court of Ohio. One of the defendants is dismissed during the trial upon evidence that he was not connected with NCR during the time named in the indictments. John Patterson, Tom Watson and the remaining twenty-seven are found guilty on all three counts. Defendants ask for a retrial.
Feb 17, 1913	Judge denies motion for retrial. Patterson, Watson and twenty-three others receive one-year sentences; three receive nine months; and one receives three months. Defendants give formal notice of an appeal.
Nov 1913	John Patterson announces Watson Sr.'s "resignation" from NCR.
Apr 1914	The Computing-Tabulating-Recording Company (C-T-R) board agrees to hire Watson but will not name him president until case is settled.
May 4, 1914	Watson starts work at C-T-R.
Fall 1914	Arguments begin before the Sixth Circuit Court of Appeals.
Mar 13, 1915	U.S. Court of Appeals for the Sixth Circuit overrules lower court's decision. The court rules that the evidence on one count was insufficient, and that neither of the other two counts should have been considered by the district court that tried the case.
Mar 15, 1915	Watson is elected president and general manager of C-T-R.
May 18, 1915	Justice Department files to have the U.S. Supreme Court review Sixth Circuit Court of Appeals judgment.
Jun 15, 1915	U.S. Supreme Court refuses to review case.
Feb 1, 1916	Almost four years after the initial indictment, the government ends litigation and dismisses the criminal case.

IBM TRADITIONAL ANNIVERSARY CELEBRATIONS

There are many dates that could have been used as an IBM anniversary date: 1888 was the founding of the Tabulating Company, 1911 was the date of incorporation of C-T-R, 1914 was the year Thomas J. Watson Sr. was hired by the C-T-R board of directors, and 1924 was when C-T-R was renamed IBM. From 1939 until the end of the century, however, 1914 was the date that was used, and it was traditionally a date to celebrate not technology, but IBM's employee-owners.

Year Being Celebrated	Date of Celebration	Event Description
	1888	Founding of Tabulating Machine Company.
	1911	C-T-R Company incorporated by Charles R. Flint.
	1914	Tom Watson Sr. joins C-T-R Company on May 4, 1914.
	1924	C-T-R Company takes on the IBM Corporation name.
1888	1925-1938	IBMers sing about the fortieth anniversary of IBM from the "Songs of The IBM."
1924	1936	IBM marks twelfth anniversary of C-T-R name change.
1914	1939	IBM celebrates the twenty-fifth anniversary of Tom Watson Sr. and his entry into the IBM Quarter Century Club, on May 4, 1939, at the New York World's Fair's IBM Day.
1914	1946	IBM celebrates "Watson Day," Watson Sr.'s thirtieth anniversary, on August 30, 1946 (postponed for two years because of World War II). Forty thousand attend event in Triple Cities.
1914	1947	IBM marks the thirty-third anniversary of Tom Watson Sr. by issuing a Watson Sr. memorial coin.
1914	1954	IBM celebrates the fortieth anniversary of Tom Watson Sr. Fifty-six thousand IBMers gather at 350 dinners in 57 countries. The dinners start on April 30, 1954, in Thailand and follow the setting sun.
1914	1964	IBM celebrates its fiftieth anniversary at New York World's Fair's "Fifty Years of Progress." Twelve thousand IBMers from thirty-two nations attend.
1914	1989	IBM celebrates its seventy-fifth Diamond Anniversary with publication of a special issue of *THINK Magazine*:"IBM A Special Company."
1911	2011	IBM celebrates its Centennial.
1914	2014	IBM Traditional Centennial.

IBM BENEFIT AND PENSION PLAN CHANGES–SUMMARY

❝ These benefits exist not because of any philanthropy on the part of myself or my executive staff or the directors and stockholders. We do it because our people do a better job everywhere. They earn all these benefits.❞

Thomas J. Watson Sr.

Event Date	Event Description
1921	First IBM Quarter Century Club
1928	IBM Suggestion Program
1934	IBM Group Life Insurance Piecework pay eliminated
1935	IBM Survivor Benefits
1937	IBM Vacation Plan
1942	Formation of Watson Fund World War II Widows and Orphans Fund
1944	IBM Health and Accident Benefit Plan
1945	IBM Retirement Plan Established
1947	IBM Permanent Disability Income Plan IBM Veteran's Benefit Plan
1956	IBM Life Insurace Plan
1984	IBM Tax Deferred 401(k) Savings Plan
1991	IBM caps retiree health liabilities Retirement multiplier revised downward
1994	IBM caps service credit at 30 years—eight years earlier than originally announced
1999	Conversion from defined-benefit to cash-balance pension plans IBM eliminates retiree health plan
2007	IBM freezes U.S. pension plan
2010	IBM eliminates UK pension plan
2013	IBM 401(k) matching funds not vested until December of each year
2014	IBM retirees (65+) moved to Extended Health

IBM BENEFIT AND PENSION PLAN CHANGES—DETAIL*

> **❝**I wish to repeat what I have said to you on every occasion of this kind: all the benefits paid for by the company for the comfort and security of yourself and your family come to you not as an inducement to work harder, but as a reward for services rendered."
>
> **Thomas J. Watson Sr.**, 1948 Broadcast to IBM Endicott employees on a loudspeaker system while they worked over their machines.
>
> **❝**We cannot do any more without putting IBM's competitiveness at risk."
>
> **Louis V. Gerstner,** April 25, 2000, Annual stockholders meeting

1914

○ Thomas J. Watson Sr.

1921

- **IBM Quarter Century Club**—An organization of IBM veterans is organized. The first meeting of the Quarter Century Club is held in Atlantic City on June 21, 1921.[1]

1928

- **IBM Suggestion Plan**—The IBM suggestion program, inaugurated in 1928, is designed to stimulate creative thinking among employees and reward them for ideas that result in reduced costs, improved quality or other contributions to better products and/or working conditions.[2]

1933

- **IBM Quarter Century Club**—Members upon qualification are provided with a $2,500 paid-up life insurance policy, gold watch and certificate of membership. (Exact date of implementation of these benefits is uncertain.)[3]

1934

- **Piecework pay eliminated**—An hourly rate basis of remuneration replaces piecework in all IBM plants at the end of 1934. It is believed that an hourly basis of pay results in a higher-quality product and establishes greater economic stability for employees.[4]

- **IBM Group Life Insurance**
  - In September, a *worldwide* $1,000 group life insurance paid-up policy is initiated.[5]
  - In December, Tom Watson Sr. declares, "So far as this company is concerned the Depression is over" and increases the paid-up life insurance policy from $1,000 to $2,000 and the minimum hourly pay by 37.5%.[6]

1935

- **IBM Survivor Benefits**—Survivor benefits added to the IBM Group Life Insurance Program.[7]

1936

- **Overtime pay**—Increased from regular pay to time and a half.[8]
- **Hourly pay increase**—Five-cents-per-hour pay raise.[9]
- **Christmas bonus**—Employees with one year of service or more receive approximately one week's pay. Those with more than six months and less than one year receive half a week's salary. This amounts to a corporate expense of roughly $130,000.[10]

1937

- **Hourly pay increase**—Five cents per hour pay raise.[11]
- **IBM Vacation Plan**
  - New paid vacation policy instituted on orders from Watson Sr. for hourly workers. (This replaces the 1936 Christmas bonus for Endicott employees—one week's vacation with pay.) Salaried workers already had a vacation policy in place "for many years." Employees with one year's continuous active service receive two weeks of paid vacation. Employees with a six-month service record receive one week of paid vacation.[12]
  - Starting in June 1937, employees are paid for six annual holidays.[13]

1940

- **Military Service**—IBM announces it will present three months' pay to every employee who has had one year's employment or more and is now in active military or naval service or enters it. Those with less than a year's employment will receive one and a half months' compensation. Payments will be made in equal monthly installments covering the employee's years of military service.[14]

1942

- **The Watson Fund**—A special reserve fund created for the benefit of employees. It is created when Tom Watson Sr. refuses to share personally in any profits derived from the production of war materials and reduces the contract rate of his percentage commission.[15]

- **Widows' and Orphans' Fund**—IBM limits its corporate profits to less than 1.5% on wartime munitions and establishes a fund for the benefit of widows and orphans of IBM employees who lost their lives in World War II.[16]

1943

- **IBM Vacation Plan**—IBM provides summer vacation option for hourly employees from July 27, 1943, through August 10, 1943, at estimated cost of $600,000.[17]

1944

- **IBM Health and Accident Benefit Plan**—Sickness and accident benefit insurance added.[18]

1945

- **IBM Retirement Plan established**[19]

    – Retirement plan pays retiring employees a minimum of $60 monthly with Social Security benefits and a maximum of $130 monthly with Social Security benefits. The IBM pension plan is coordinated with the federal Social Security program. A married man retiring at age sixty-five receives a total of $155 under the IBM plan and Social Security. This includes credit for his wife if she is still alive.

    – The retirement plan requires that any beneficiary shall have been an employee of the company for ten years by the time he reaches his sixty-fifth birthday. Those with shorter periods of service are to be handled on an individual basis.

    – All IBM employees get the same retirement income regardless of their position or earnings while they were with the company. It is presumed that those with larger earnings during their period of service will have been better able to prepare for their own retirement.

    – The IBM Retirement Plan is funded in part by the Watson Fund established during World War II and carried on the IBM annual report through 1958.[20]

- **Benefits Summary** (summarized by Tom Watson Sr. to twenty thousand IBMers in September 1945)

    – Two weeks of paid vacation and paid holidays.

    – Illness benefit up to six months.

- Paid life insurance up to a maximum of $25,000.
- $500 gift for Quarter Century Club members.
- Payment of one-fourth their peacetime salaries to men during their period of service.
- Education programs.
- Recreational facilities at the company's country clubs.

1946

- **IBM Hospitalization Plan**—A Hospitalization Plan for employees is implemented.[21]

1947

- **IBM Vacation Plan**—Starting in January employees with the company for more than ten years will get a third week of vacation with pay in line with an enlarged benefit program.[22]
- **IBM Retirement System**—These pension increases are paid out of the Watson Fund: [23]

  - An increase of $17.50 per month after 43 years of service, bringing the total monthly payment to $182.50.
  - An increase of $14.00 per month after 40 years of service, bringing the total monthly payment to $164.
  - An increase of $10.50 per month after 35 years of service, bringing the total monthly payment to $145.50.
  - An increase of $7.00 per month after 30 years of service, bringing the total monthly payment to $127.
  - An increase of $3.50 per month after 25 years of service, bringing the total monthly payment to $108.50.
  - Extension of the retirement plan to embrace workers who retire after 20 years or more of service but before they reach the 63-year retirement age, so that they may receive a prorated pension at age 65.

- **IBM Veteran's Benefit Program**—Extended to provide for payment of pensions to children of employees who gave their lives in World War II until the children reach age 21 (previously age 19).

- **IBM Total and Permanent Disability Income Plan** — Extension of the retirement plan to embrace employees retired because of total permanent disability, previously handled on an individual basis.

- **IBM Retirement** System — IBM extends retirement system to Canada and assumes the responsibility of paying $517,185 as the estimated cost of employees' service prior to introduction of the retirement plan.[24]

1948

- **IBM Retirement System**[25]

  - IBM provides paid-up insurance policies for retiring workers: $500 for all employees retiring with ten years of continuous service, with $50 per year added for each additional year of service, so that at forty-five years the insurance amounts to $2,250.

  - Dependents of employees who retire under the IBM retirement plan are also covered.

  - Monthly pension increases are provided for employees with service records of twenty-five, thirty and forty years and increases are paid for from the Watson Fund.

1950

- **IBM Veteran's Benefit Program** — With the United Nations-initiated action in Korea, the company's benefits for employees in military service are reinstated. Members of the IBM organization with the company for one year or more who enter the armed forces of the United States receive the equivalent of three months' compensation, paid in equal monthly payments, during each year of military leave of absence, up to a maximum payment of $1,000 per year.

- **IBM Family Hospitalization Plan** — Benefits are extended to the wives and children of employees in military service.

- **The IBM Widows' and Orphans' Plan** — Continued from World War II, benefits the widows and children of IBM employees who die while serving in the armed forces. The company pays widows and children an amount equal to that paid by the United States government under the Widows and Orphans Act. Payments by the company to the widow continue for her lifetime or until remarriage. Payments by the company for a child continue until age twenty-one.[26]

1951

- **IBM Retirement Plan**

  - Pension increases range from $15 to $25 per month in the amounts to be received by retired employees, including Social Security. A ten-year employee will receive $75 a month under the revised schedule (an increase of $15) and a twenty-year employee will draw $115 (an increase of $25). The new pension scale goes up to $240 a month for forty-five-year employees.[27]

  - Payments in 1951 to the pension trustee total $2,543,068, of which $1,098,584 is paid under the IBM Retirement Plan and $1,444,484 [56.8%] from the Watson Fund for Supplementing the IBM Retirement Plan.[28]

1952

- **IBM Retirement Plan** — Payments in 1952 to the trustee total $3,014,811 of which $1,466,868 is paid under the IBM Retirement Plan and $1,547,943 [51.3%] from the Watson Fund for Supplementing the IBM Retirement Plan.[29]

1953

- **IBM Retirement Plan** — Payments in 1953 to the trustee totaled $3,642,070, of which $2,069,333 is paid under the IBM Retirement Plan and $1,572,737 [43.2%] from the Watson Fund for Supplementing the IBM Retirement Plan.[30]

1954 (announced on December 31, 1953, by Tom Watson Sr.)[31]

- **IBM Vacation Plan** — Number of paid holidays increases from six to seven.

- **IBM Sickness and Accident Plan** — Payments to hourly rated employees absent because of sickness or accident doubled to $6 daily for the first three days. Full wages or salary will be paid from the third day to the end of six months.

- **IBM Family Hospital Plan**

  - Increased from a maximum of $8 per day to $10 for room and board during hospitalization up to 35 days. For other hospital charges, the allowance is increased from $80 to as high as $100.

  - Employees and families are covered for hospital benefits from the first day of employment instead of after six months' service.

- The plan covers all employees, dependent wives or husbands and their children under eighteen.

- **IBM Retirement Plan**

  - As of December 1, 1953, retirement benefits for those with ten or more years are increased $10 per month under the IBM Retirement Plan, supplemented by the Watson Fund. New monthly payments range from $85 including Social Security for ten years of service to $250 including Social Security for forty-five years of service.

  - During 1954 payments to the trustee totaled $4,005,622, of which $2,772,291 was paid under the IBM Retirement Plan and $1,233,331 [30.7%] from the Watson Fund for Supplementing the IBM Retirement Plan.[32]

- **IBM Suggestion Plan** — Maximum individual award for employee's suggestions doubled to $5,000.

1956 (outlined by Tom Watson Sr. at the annual shareholder's meeting in April)

- **Major Medical Protection** — Coverage to a maximum of $10,000. (The previous plan provided up to $10 a day for a maximum of 35 days for hospital room and board for any one ailment in any twelve-month period, and up to $100 for other hospital services.) Under the new plan, when an employee or any covered member of his family incurs expenses exceeding the hospitalization payments, he will receive additional benefits of 75% of all such charges over $300 up to a maximum of $10,000. An employee incurring hospital, surgical and medical expenses of $5,000 in connection with a serious illness, for instance, would receive $3,637.50 under the new plan, compared to $450 under the older program.[33]

- **IBM Vacation Plan** — Pays for seven holidays each year. An employee with six to twelve months' service receives one week's vacation with full pay; from one to ten years, two weeks' vacation with full pay; from ten to twenty-five years, three weeks' vacation with full pay; and after twenty-five years, four weeks' vacation with full pay. The fourth week may be deferred and accumulated to a total of five weeks, making possible an extended vacation of nine weeks.

- **IBM Life Insurance Plan** — Starts at $1,000 at the end of one month's service. At the end of one year it is increased to $3,000, and from one to five years it is increased $3,000 per year, so that at the end of five years of continuous service the employee has $15,000 of life insurance. It is increased $1,000 a year for the next five years, so that at the end of ten years of continuous service every employee has $20,000 of life insurance. After the tenth year, equal annual increases are made so that when the employee joins the Quarter Century Club he has $25,000 of life insurance.

- **IBM Retiree Life Insurance Plan** — Retired employees receive paid-up life insurance policies from $500 for ten years of continuous service to $2,250 for forty-five years of continuous service.

- **IBM Sickness and Accident Pay Plan** — Hourly employees receive $6 per day for the first three working days of absence due to illness; beginning with the fourth consecutive working day absent, the company pays full wages or salary for six months. At the end of six months, each case is treated individually depending on physical condition and other factors surrounding the case.

- **IBM Retirement Plan**

  - Provides employees retiring at age 65, with ten or more years' continuous service, with a retirement income for life, based on length of service, ranging from $110 per month for ten years of continuous service to $275 per month for 45 years, both figures including Social Security.

  - Under the new retirement formula, which is based on earnings as well as length of service, a retiring employee receives whichever retirement income is greater — the one computed exclusively on his length of service or the one computed on both length of service and earnings — but no retirement income shall be greater than $25,000 a year, including the employee's Social Security benefit.

  - During 1956 payments to the trustee totaled $6,604,520, of which $5,290,182 was paid under the IBM Retirement Plan and $1,314,338 [19.9%] from the Watson Fund for Supplementing the IBM Retirement Plan.

- **IBM Suggestion Plan** — The IBM Suggestion Plan (by 1956) awards in proportion to the value of the suggestion submitted. $10 is the minimum award and $5,000 is the maximum award.[34]

1956

❂ **Thomas J. Watson Jr.**

1957

- **IBM Suggestion Plan** — IBM Suggestion Plan payments are $777,473.19 in 1957. IBM accepts 27,978 of 152,463 suggestions. Over the previous five years IBM paid out $2,684,695 in awards.[35]

1958

- **IBM Salary Plan** — Twenty thousand IBM U.S. regular hourly rated employees placed on salary.[36]
- **IBM Employee Stock Purchase Plan** — IBM employee stock purchase plan started.[37]
- **Military Service** — Military service is applied as IBM "time served" when returning to IBM, with full credit for continuous military service (exact date of implementation uncertain).[38]

1959

- **IBM Retirement Plan**[39] — Retirement at 65 with five years of service (ten years previously required) and at 55 with fifteen years of service.
- **IBM Major Medical and Hospitalization Plans**[40]
  - Annual medical deductible is reduced.
  - Age of children's medical coverage is raised from 19 to 23 years.
- **IBM Matching Grants** — IBM matches company grants to colleges and universities.
- **IBM Miscellaneous Benefits** — IBM employee's orchestra, mixed chorus and men's glee club no longer funded.[41]

1960

- **Vacation Plan Changes**[42]
  - Employees with less than one year receive one day's vacation for each full month beginning with the second month of employment.
  - Employees with one to eight years receive two weeks.
  - Starting with the eighth year, employees receive three weeks.
  - Starting with the twentieth year, employees receive four weeks.
  - Starting with the twenty-fifth year, employees receive five weeks.

1961

- **IBM Suggestion Plan**—The IBM Suggestion Plan awards a $25 minimum and $75,000 maximum, with the award representing 15% of the company first year's savings on the suggestion.[43]

1971

○ **T. Vincent Learson**

1973

○ **Frank T. Cary**

1981

○ **John R. Opel**

July 1983

- **IBM Tax Deferred Savings Plan (TDSP)**—Employee is allowed to defer up to 5% of his or her salary.[44]

1984

- **IBM Tax Deferred Savings Plan (TDSP)**—IBM adds 30 cents for every dollar contributed up to 4% of the employee's salary.[45]

1985

○ **John F. Akers**

1985

- **IBM Tax Deferred Savings Plan (TDSP)**—Employee is allowed to contribute up to 8% of compensation and IBM matches 30 cents for every dollar contributed up to 5% of the employee's salary.[46]

February 1985

- **IBM Suggestion Plan**—Maximum award raised from $100,000 to $150,000.[47]

January 1991

- **IBM Pension Plan**
  - The retirement multiplier revised from 1.50% to 1.35%.

- Service and earnings base year period reduced from ten years to five years.
- Minimum benefit formula base year period shortened from five years to three years.
- Service formula discontinued.
- Thirty-year service credit maximum to be implemented January 1, 2001. (This is moved up in a later announcement to December 31, 1993.)
- Personal retirement provision (PRP) feature added to IBM Retirement Plan.
- Full unreduced benefits available at thirty years of service. Retirement reductions are 2% for each year prior to attaining thirty years of service or age sixty, whichever is earlier.

December 1991

- **IBM Retirement Health Plan** — IBM caps its retiree health liabilities: the company pays the full premium up to $7,000 for those under age sixty-five and up to $3,000 for those ages sixty-five and over. The caps will apply to IBM employees retiring after December 31, 1991. Given current trends in health care costs, the company estimates that these limits will be reached by the late 1990s, when they will consider various options.[48]

January 1992

- **IBM Pension Plan**
  - Service and earnings base year updated to 1987–1991.
  - New minimum benefit base updated to 1989–1991 (applies to all employees who retire on January 31, 1992, or later and those whose retirement is effective in 1991).

March 1993

- **IBM Pension Plan**
  - Service and earnings formula base years moved to 1989–1993. Minimum benefit formula base years moved to 1991–1993.
  - Elimination of preretirement education.

1993

○ **Louis V. Gerstner**

January 1994

- **IBM Pension Plan**

  - On December 31, 1993, eight years earlier than previously announced, IBM implements a thirty-year cap on service or actual service. This was previously announced in January 1991 to go into effect on January 1, 2001.

  - Service and earnings formula base years moved to 1990–1994.

  - Minimum benefit formula base years moved to 1992–1994.

January 1995

- **IBM Pension Plan**

  - IBM Retirement Plan changed to pension credit formula (PCF). Under the new PCF plan the rate of future accruals is decreased.

  - Annual PRP allocations discontinued, but balances continue to accrue 4% interest.

March 1996

- **IBM Pension Plan**—Retirement bridge leave of absence discontinued for employees not within five years of retirement eligibility as of March 1, 1996. However, a resource reduction program may provide a retirement bridge leave of absence.

January 1997

- **IBM Pension Plan**

  - Five-year service and earnings formula base years moved to 1992–1996. Minimum benefit formula base years moved to 1994–1996. (Ten year service and earnings formula base years remain 1985–1994.)

  - Preretirement Spouse Protection (PRSP) is extended to qualified domestic partners of those active employees in a committed same-gender relationship.

January 1998

- **IBM Pension Plan**—A total benefit may not be taken as a lump-sum payment unless the total present value of the plan benefit is $5,000 or less (formerly $3,500).

July 1999

- **IBM Pension Plan**—Personal pension account (PPA) effective. This cash balance account plan replaces the IBM Pension Plan—prior plan for most employees.

2002

⊙ **Samuel J. Palmisano**

January 2005

- **IBM Pension Plan**—IBM drops defined-benefit pensions and no longer offers pensions to workers hired after January 1, 2005, who will be offered only an enhanced 401(k) matching 100% of an employee's contributions up to 6% of pay. New workers can buy disability insurance that will cover their contributions if they are temporarily disabled.[49]

December 2007

- **IBM Pension Plan**—IBM stops contributing to its pension fund and puts in place a hard freeze. Pension benefits are locked in place, based on salary and length of service. The accrual of benefits stops, meaning future raises or additional years with the company will not signify bigger pension checks.

- **IBM Tax Deferred Savings 401K Plan** (TDSP)[50]
  - IBM increases its contribution to its 401(k) plans and increases the percentage of employees' contributions that it matches, to 6% of salary. Certain employees are eligible to receive more: for employees with the pre-1999 defined-benefit pension plan, IBM matches contributions of up to 6% of an employee's salary and adds 4% on top. For employees in the pension plan that ran through 2004, IBM matches 6% and adds 2%, and for those hired in 2005 or later, the company matches 5% and adds 1%.

April 2010

- **IBM Pension Plan** — With about 28% of employees still on a defined-benefit plan, the IBM UK defined-benefit plan is closed to further accruals. Employees can no longer build up additional benefits under the plan, and until then, salary increases will no longer count toward the plan. Employees have the option of joining the defined-contribution plan.[51]

2011

◑ **Virginia M. Rometty**

January 2013

- **IBM TDSP Plan** — To receive the IBM 401(k) matching contribution an employee must be employed on December 15 of the current year. For eligible IBMers, the IBM match and automatic contribution will be deposited to the 401(k) account on December 31, 2013 (and on the last business day of each subsequent year).[52]

January 2014

- **IBM Retirement Health Plan** — IBM United States retirees (sixty-five-plus years of age) on Medicare moved to extended health plan.[53]

Endnotes

1 Thomas J. Watson Sr., *Men — Minutes — Money* (IBM Corporation, New York, 1934), p. 64, reprinted with permission of IBM.

2 "Their Suggestion Award — $56,031," *Kingston Daily Freeman*, May 18, 1961.

3 "6,900 IBM Employees to Get Policies," *Binghamton Press*, September 26, 1934.

4 "Heart Attack Fatal Today to IBM Board Chairman," *Kingston Daily Freeman*, June 19, 1956, p. 16.

5 "6,900 IBM Employees to Get Policies," *Binghamton Press*, September 26, 1934.

6 "Increases Pay," *Brooklyn Daily Eagle*, December 23, 1934.

7 IBM online archives.

8 "Three Thousand IBM Workers on Hourly Basis to Get Paid Vacations," *Binghamton Press*, April 22, 1937.

9 Ibid.

10 Ibid.

11 Ibid.

12 Ibid.

13 "Three Thousand IBM Workers Back from Vacation," *Binghamton Press*, August 9, 1937.

14 "Pay for Men in the Service," *New York Times*, December 24, 1940.

15 "Good Human Relations, Organic Part of IBM Make-up," *Kingston Daily Freeman*, November 2, 1956, p. 16-C.

16 "Heart Attack Fatal Today to IBM Board Chairman," *Kingston Daily Freeman*, June 19, 1956, p. 16.

17 "IBM to Give Employees $600,000 in Vacation Pay," *Binghamton Press*, July 27, 1943.

18 "IBM Still Has 60 Million in War Contracts," *Binghamton Press*, April 25, 1945, p. 17.

19 "New Retirement Plan Pays $60–$130 Monthly Costs Million a Year," *Binghamton Press*, September 15, 1945, pp. 3, 5.

20 IBM 1959 annual report.

21 IBM online archives.

22 "IBM Vacation Pay Nearly $1,000,000," *Binghamton Press*, July 23, 1947, p. 5.

23 "IBM Hikes Employee Benefits," *Binghamton Press*, August 13, 1947, p. 25.

24 "IBM Net Profits Exceed 1946," *Binghamton Press*, March 10, 1948.

25 "IBM Provides Paid-Up Insurance Policies for Retiring Workers," *Binghamton Press*, February 5, 1948.

26 "IBM Benefits to Employees Outlined By Chairman at Annual Meeting," *Kingston Daily Freeman*, November 2, 1956, p. 11-B.

27 "Pensions Boosted by IBM," *Binghamton Press*, December 30, 1950.

28 "IBM Production at New Peak," *Binghamton Press*, February 27, 1952.

29 Ibid.

30 "IBM Hits Record Net Profits for 1953 After Taxes," *Binghamton Press*, February 19, 1954.

31 "New Benefits Are Announced for All IBM Employees," *Kingston Daily Freeman*, December 31, 1953.

32 "IBM Gives Net Income for 1954," *Kingston Daily Freeman*, February 1, 1955.

33 "IBM Adds to Benefits for U.S. Employees," *Binghamton Press*, April 5, 1956, p. 19.

34 "Good Human Relations, Organic Part of IBM Make-up," *Kingston Daily Freeman*, November 2, 1956.

35 "IBM Payment for Ideas $777,473.19," *Binghamton Press*, January 27, 1958.

36 "IBM Salaries Workers," *Geneva Times*, January 31, 1958.

37 "IBM Employees Get Common Stock Plan," *Amsterdam Evening Recorder*, April 2, 1958.

38 "IBM Oswego Plant Dedication and Open House," *Binghamton Press*, June 17, 1958.

39 "Retirement Possible at 55," *Kingston Daily Freeman*, April 2, 1959.

40 Ibid.

41 "IBM/E.J. Paternal Shield Lifts Higher," *Binghamton Press*, February 15, 1959.

42 "IBM Liberalizes Vacation Policy," *Binghamton Press*, January 4, 1960.

43 "Their Suggestion Award — $56,031," *Kingston Daily Freeman*, May 18, 1961.

44 From IBM Savings Plan document dated January 1, 2005.

45 From IBM Tax Deferred Savings Plan (TDSP) Calculator.

46 Ibid.

47 John F. Akers, IBM Suggestion Plan memorandum to IBM managers, February 4, 1985.

48 Employee Benefit Research Institute (EBRI), issue brief number 112, March 1991, p. 16.

49 Albert B. Crenshaw, "IBM Stops Offering Cash-Balance Pension," *Washington Post*, December 9, 2004.

50 Stephen Shankland, "IBM Freezes Pension, Switches to 401(k)," CNET News, January 5, 2006.

51 Cade Metz, "IBM UK Snuffs 'Final Salary' Pensions," *Register*, July 7, 2009.

52 Randy McDonald, IBM senior vice president of human resources, e-mail to IBM employees, December 5, 2012.

53 Sarah Frier, "IBM Moves Retirees to Insurance Exchange as Costs Rise," Bloomberg, September 7, 2013.

APPENDIX F

THE
$1,000-A-DAY
MAN

The Revenue Act of 1934 required the U.S. Treasury to publish the names of corporate officials making more than $15,000 in salaries, commissions and bonuses. Not included were incomes from dividends, proprietorships, partnerships, rents or royalties; neither did the act account for salaries received from multiple corporations. Many Hollywood stars formed corporations to produce their movies and then received their earnings as dividends. The report did not measure wealth, as the nation's richest families—the Du Ponts, the Rockefellers, the Fords and the Morgans—earned their incomes through capital investments. With the advent of World War II, an individual earning a $100,000 salary and producing vital war materials could be brought into the public eye while another individual receiving $1,000,000 from investments and paying little in taxes to support the war would go unnoticed.

At times the approximately eleven-hundred page report listed almost fifty thousand individuals from more than eight thousand corporations. It could be a chaotic scene when the report was released, as reporters pushed and shoved to be the first in line for a front-page story—revealing the year's highest paid individual, industrialist, movie mogul, entertainer or woman. The chairman of the House Ways and Means Committee, after seeing the commotion with the release of the 1936 report, temporarily suspended access, commenting that the list might get "disarranged or lost."*

The report would also be released and updated as corporations closed out their fiscal years, so the highest paid individual could be very fluid. A business section headline of the *New York Post* on May 6, 1936, read, "Watson's Pay of $303,813 Tops '35 List." Less than thirty days later, the headline of the same paper read, "Sloan Highest Paid Executive with $374,505." The final winner was William Randolph Hearst.

In April 1942, Watson asked the board of directors to modify his employment contract. Refusing to profit personally from the manufacture of war munitions, he reduced his profit-sharing compensation from 5% to 2.5%. He made the new contract retroactive to 1941. It was later determined that it was

We, the employes of International Business Machines Corporation, take this opportunity to express publicly our sincere appreciation to Thomas J. Watson, our President, and to our Board of Directors for their thoughtfulness of our welfare and for the many privileges and benefits which we have received.

Their vision and leadership has made possible for us continuous employment with an assured income.

They have provided for us a safe, clean, healthy workplace.

They have provided us with unlimited opportunities for advancement, and have established an educational program to help us progress with the business.

They have established a sense of security by providing life insurance for us.

They have increased our opportunities for social and sport activities through the medium of the I. B. M. Country Club and the I. B. M. musical organizations.

Other benefits, too numerous to mention, have been ours.

On this, the most joyful holiday season we have ever had, we send heartfelt greetings to Thomas J. Watson and our Board of Directors, and wish them the Merry Christmas and Happy New Year which they justly deserve.

THE EMPLOYES OF INTERNATIONAL BUSINESS MACHINES CORPORATION
ENDICOTT, N. Y.

BY:
R. H. Vanderpoel   George Burnett   Martin Berg
Herbert Page   A. Schweckendieck   George Savage
Lewis Golden

EMPLOYES' COMMITTEE

IBM employees ran this 1935 advertisement thanking their $1,000-a-day CEO.

---

* In 1940 the salary limit was changed from $15,000 to $75,000, reducing the list to between 400 and 800 individuals. This reduced much of the confusion.

too difficult to determine the increase in general business attributable to the war, so he requested that his commissions not exceed that of 1939, when the company had had no war business.[1]

Reading newspapers of the time, it appears that Watson Sr.'s salary was more fodder for letters to the editor than it was the subject matter of serious editorials. It is also interesting that after the ups and downs of his salary over twenty-two years Watson's earnings (including commissions) in 1951 were down 10% while IBM's revenue was up by more than 1,500%. One has to wonder if today's authors who poke fun at Watson Sr.'s earnings would be satisfied with their salary if it remained flat for seventeen years and, when commissions were considered, decreased over twenty-two years.

Thomas J. Watson Sr.'s Salary 1929–1951*

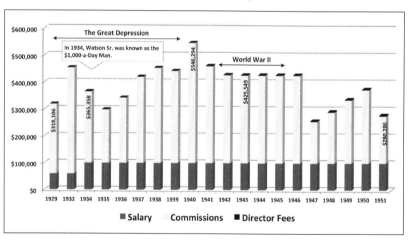

---

* There are some historical gaps in earnings in 1930, 1931, 1933 and after 1951.

Comparing Two Executives' Net Income in 1942 [2]

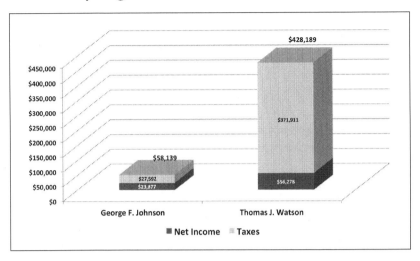

$428,189

$450,000
$400,000
$350,000
$300,000
$250,000 $371,911
$200,000
$150,000
$100,000 $58,139
$50,000 $27,592 $56,278
$0 $23,877

George F. Johnson   Thomas J. Watson

■ Net Income ■ Taxes

Endnotes

1 "Thomas J. Watson Received $428,189 from IBM in 1942," *Binghamton Press*, April 7, 1943, p. 17.

2 "Johnsons' Salaries Modest; What Taxes Do to Them and T.J. Watson Personally," *Binghamton Press*, April 17, 1943, p. 5.

IBM MANAGEMENT PRINCIPLES[1]

Managers Must Lead Effectively

Our success depends on intelligent and aggressive management which is sensitive to the need for making an enthusiastic partner of every individual in the organization. This requires that managers:

- Provide the kind of leadership that will motivate employees to do their jobs in a superior way.
- Meet frequently with all their people.
- Have the courage to question decisions and policies; have the vision to see the needs of the Company as well as the division and department.
- Plan for the future by keeping an open mind to new ideas, whatever the source.

Obligations to Stockholders

IBM has obligations to its stockholders whose capital has created our jobs. These require us to:

- Take care of the property our stockholders have entrusted to us.

- Provide an attractive return on invested capital.

- Exploit opportunities for continuing profitable growth.

Fair Deal for the Supplier

We want to deal fairly and impartially with suppliers of goods and services. We should:

- Select suppliers according to the quality of their products or services, their general reliability and competitiveness of price.

- Recognize the legitimate interests of both supplier and IBM when negotiating a contract; administer such contracts in good faith.

- Avoid suppliers becoming unduly dependent on IBM.

IBM Should be a Good Corporate Citizen

We accept our responsibilities as a corporate citizen in community, national and world affairs; we serve our interest best when we serve the public interest. We believe that the immediate and long-term public interest is best served by a system of competing enterprises. Therefore, we believe we should compete vigorously, but in a spirit of fair play, with respect for our competitors, and with respect for the law. In communities where IBM facilities are located, we do our utmost to help create an environment in which people want to work and live. We acknowledge our obligation as a business institution to help improve the quality of the society we are part of. We want to be in the forefront of those companies which are working to make our world a better place.

Endnote

1   Thomas J. Watson Jr., *Thirty Years of Management Briefings* (IBM Corporation, Armonk, New York, 1988) pp. 128–131, reprinted with permission of IBM.

ACKNOWLEDGMENTS

In the days of knights and kings swords were forged. They were tempered in fire. The smith, though, did not know if the metal was true, as one blade looked like another, until it went into battle. Failure there meant death. So the smiths learned to test the strength of the sword upon a large stone. The blade would be drawn and smashed against this rock. Weaker swords shattered, but a true work of art did not fail. It was a test by a touchstone. On the inside of my wife's wedding ring it reads, "To my touchstone." She has never failed in that role.

My editor adapted his style of editing for a neophyte author working on only his second book. I asked him to make me a better writer. I know it was painful. I hope, as much for him as for myself, that this book achieves success. If it does, it is a tribute to his work; if it doesn't, it will be through no fault of his.

Thanks to Rivkah for her inspired drawings in this book, especially *Musical Chairs*. I don't know any artist who could better convey such emotion in such a simple drawing.

Thanks to Princeton Books for finding an old, out-of-print book I needed. Thanks to Old Fulton Post Cards (http://fultonhistory.com) and their commitment to providing information that can't be found anywhere else.

Thanks to the thousands of IBMers who have contributed their thoughts on LinkedIn forums, in personal e-mails and in interviews during times that were sometimes personally painful. I need to extend a special thanks to Kathi Cooper, Janet Krueger and every IBMer who fought the cash-balance decision. Without the stand they took, this book would have never been published; but, even so, there are still many working today who should be retired.

INDEX

Made in the USA
Middletown, DE
03 May 2015